Guide to
Performance Assessment
for California Teachers
(PACT)

Judy Lombardi

California State University at Northridge

Boston   Columbus   Indianapolis   New York   San Francisco
Upper Saddle River   Amsterdam   Cape Town   Dubai   London   Madrid
Milan   Munich   Paris   Montreal   Toronto   Delhi   Mexico City   Sao Paulo
Sydney   Hong Kong   Seoul   Singapore   Taipei   Tokyo

Series Editor: Kelly Villella Canton
Series Editorial Assistant: Annalea Manalili
Senior Marketing Manager: Darcy Betts
Vice President, Director of Marketing: Quinn Perkson
Production Editor: Paula Carroll
Editorial Production Service: Publishers' Design and Production Services, Inc.
Manufacturing Buyer: Megan Cochran
Electronic Composition: Publishers' Design and Production Services, Inc.
Interior Design: Publishers' Design and Production Services, Inc.
Cover Designer: Linda Knowles

For related titles and support materials, visit our online catalog at www.pearsonhighered.com.

Between the time website information is gathered and then published, it is not unusual for some sites to have closed. Also, the transcription of URLs can result in typographical errors. The publisher would appreciate notification where these errors occur so that they may be corrected in subsequent editions.

Cataloging-in-Publication data is on file but unavailable at press time.

10 9 8 7 6 5 4 3 2 1   14 13 12 11 10

www.pearsonhighered.com

ISBN-10: 0132143143
ISBN-13: 978013243141

This book is dedicated to my dear son Richie;
to my grandfather, who inspired me to get an education;
and to my family, whose love and support
are the wind beneath my wings.

CHAPTER 2

The PACT Teaching Event   39

CHAPTER 3

Understanding Academic Language   57

The purpose of this book is to help you understand the Performance Assessment for California Teachers (PACT). We will explore several areas of PACT: the research behind it, definitions and descriptions of PACT, examples of the PACT Teaching Event, academic language, an explanation of how the Teaching Event is scored, and next steps for further study and review.

If you are a preservice or student teacher, faculty member, or teacher preparation program administrator in a PACT-aligned institution, here you will find a helpful overview of the PACT format and features. The PACT website at http://pacttpa.org is a wonderful repository of PACT information, but no single text exists that brings all the key information together the way this book does.

This text should be read as a primer on PACT essentials, organized around the topics candidates most frequently ask about PACT. Although the foundations of the assessment itself are clearly presented by PACT-aligned institutions, each teacher education program has its own procedures and policies for submission and score dissemination. Only state-trained scorers are allowed to evaluate the PACT Teaching Event, and the state holds regular benchmark sessions and annual conferences to keep participants updated.

Candidates who first encounter PACT frequently ask: Where did it come from? How was PACT created and developed? The Introduction, Chapter 1, and Chapter 2 address these questions, as well as the rich history of teacher performance assessment in California. Chapter 2 also closely examines the PACT Teaching Event for candidates, describing its primary sections and requirements with examples.

One of the areas with which candidates—and sometimes, faculty—struggle is academic language. Chapter 3 explains what academic language is, why it is important, and how to apply academic language effectively to the PACT Teaching Event. The language demands of school that are placed on learners can be better understood and integrated into classroom practice, by implementing the ideas in Chapter 3, Understanding Academic Language.

Candidates also ask: How will I be evaluated? What are the major areas of the PACT scoring form? Chapter 4 breaks down the scoring process, rubrics, and the big ideas behind the rubrics.

Chapter 5 provides next steps for PACT, answering the questions, Where do we go from here? What features of PACT are most useful to strengthen teacher preparation programs? How can student teaching be made more applicable to real classroom practice? Chapter 5 suggests new directions for exciting research and further study in these areas.

Even if you have not yet heard of PACT, when you finish reading the information presented here, you will have a clear understanding of what PACT is, including how and why it was developed.

So, welcome aboard on this exciting journey! Join me, as we explore a new form of teacher performance assessment, developed by some of the best education experts in the country. First, we will examine the research on teacher performance assessment, and then we will continue our journey, exploring all the various features of PACT.

● Acknowledgments

Thank you to the following reviewers for their helpful comments: Richard Jon Battaglia, California Lutheran University; Sandy Buczynski, University of San Diego; Jamal A. Cooks, San Francisco State University; Christina Giguiere, University of California, Irvine; Gustavo Gonzales, San Diego State University; Linda S. Nowell, California State University, Sacramento; and Joy Springer, Pepperdine University.

Research on Teacher Performance and PACT

What is quality teacher performance? How can education experts describe what effective teachers do well, and what preservice teachers need to know? How can teacher educators improve current and future teacher preparation programs and practices? Research findings on teacher performance assessment have helped respond to these questions and indicate next steps for further study and practice.

Teacher performance assessment from the 1990s to now has been a robust and sometimes controversial process, from the California Teacher Performance Assessment to the Florida clinical education model to National Board certification and aspects of federal No Child Left Behind legislation. All states now have some kind of standards-based performance requirement as part of their teacher credentialing process.

How California Teacher Assessment Reform Began

In 1998, the California legislature passed Senate Bill 2042, commonly referred to by educators as SB2042. This legislative mandate called for teacher candidates to complete a teaching performance assessment in order to obtain a preliminary teaching credential. Additional coursework and on-the-job training were required within five years of completing the preliminary level to achieve the clear, lifetime, professional credential.

Within the California plan, teacher preparation programs were provided two options. Programs could either implement the Teacher Performance Assessment (TPA) designed by the state in consultation with the Education Testing Service (ETS), or develop their own TPA, as long as it fulfilled the state's Assessment Quality Standards. As a result, the current version of PACT, or Performance Assessment for California Teachers, emerged in the spring of 2003 from a 12-institution consortium spearheaded by education experts at Stanford University (Chung, 2008). PACT-aligned institutions now credential 29.2 percent of newly credentialed teachers in California (Pecheone, 2007).

According to Ruth Chung, a key PACT researcher at Stanford, along with Ray Pecheone, Linda Darling-Hammond, and Kendyll Stansbury, the PACT Teaching Event emanated from "studies of pre-service teachers who have completed a TPA, portfolio assessments in particular, [which] have examined learning outcomes for teachers and have generally found positive effects on their learning [based on the research of] Anderson & DeMeulle, 1998; Lyons, 1996, 1998a, 1998b, 1999; Snyder, Lippincott, & Bower, 1998; Stone, 1998; Whitford, Ruscoe, & Fickel, 2000" (Chung, 2008, p. 1).

Researchers involved with PACT first studied state and national portfolio assessments for preservice teachers. Based on their findings, they decided to update, revamp, and infuse existing assessments with new depth and analysis through artifacts, commentary, and video clips. As a result, the PACT Teaching Event was born.

The centerpiece of the performance assessment, the Teaching Event, or TE, is a subject-specific portfolio of teaching. The TE is submitted in a teacher candidate's preparation program at a PACT-aligned institution, as part of the capstone experience in student teaching. An essential goal of the PACT consortium was that the TE not only reflect preservice teachers' strengths and challenges but also serve as a springboard for program improvement and reflective teaching (Pecheone & Chung, 2006, Chung, 2008).

The Teaching Event selected by the PACT consortium is a standardized set of integrated tasks in **planning, instruction, assessment, and reflection** built around a unified learning segment of approximately one week. The TE also addresses the **context for learning** (target population and learner needs) and the **academic language** demands placed on learners (http://pacttpa.org [PACT, 2008]). The PACT TE and scoring rubrics are both subject-specific and aligned with the California Teacher Performance Expectations, or TPEs. (See Chapter 1 for a discussion of the TPEs, Chapter 2 for a description of the PACT Teaching Event, and Chapter 4 for more details on the scoring form.)

Based on pilot studies, focus groups, and data from two surveys, the findings on the implementation of the TE in PACT-aligned institutions yielded results that could be generalized to other teacher preparation programs. Comparisons were made on teacher candidate experiences within and across programs. Self-reports, observational data, and candidate debriefing helped to guide the process of revising the TE and scoring form as needed, based on feedback and implementation results from early adopter institutions (Chung, 2008).

The No Child Left Behind (NCLB) Act, federal legislation enacted in 2001, addressed three areas of education, as it (1) reauthorized a number of federal programs to improve public school performance, (2) required all public schools that receive federal funds to administer a statewide standardized test annually to all students, and (3) specified that states must report their progress in an annual report card to the U.S. Department of Education. No Child Left Behind enacts the principles of standards-based education reform and is based on the belief that setting high standards, requiring accountability, and establishing measurable goals can improve individual outcomes in education (www.ed.gov/nclb/landing.jhtml [No Child Left Behind, 2008a]).

No Child Left Behind also calls for highly qualified teachers for all students and specifies the minimum qualifications needed by teachers: a bachelor's degree, full state teacher certification, and demonstration of subject-matter competency for each subject taught (www.ed.gov/nclb/landing.jhtml [No Child Left Behind, 2008a]). The NCLB law leaves it to individual states to devise their own teacher performance assessments and "puts a special emphasis on implementing education programs and practices that have been clearly demonstrated to be effective through rigorous scientific research" (www.ed.gov/teachers/nclbguide/nclb-teachers-toolkit .pdf [No Child Left Behind, 2008a, p. 16]).

● Research on the PACT Model of Teacher Performance Assessment

Three primary types of research on the TPAs, including the PACT consortium's own ongoing research, informed the PACT process:

1. Teacher self-report studies, based on interviews, surveys, and focus groups on teacher experiences (King, 1991; Athanases, 1994; Tracz, Sienty, & Mata, 1994; Tracz et al., 1995; Rotberg, Futrell, & Lieberman, 1998; Stone, 1998; Sato, 2000; cited in Chung, 2008, p. 1)
2. Portfolio artifact studies on reflections, course papers, and evidence used by teacher preparation programs to assess candidates (Lyons, 1998a, 1999; Snyder, Lippincott, & Bower, 1998; cited in Chung, 2008, p. 1)
3. Group comparison studies, in regard to candidates who completed a TPA versus those who did not, especially those from the National Board for Professional Teaching Standards studies and who reported learning outcomes and student achievement gains for classroom learners (Bond, Smith, Baker, & Hattie, 2000; Lustick & Sykes, 2006; Cavalluzzo, 2004; Vandevoort, Amrein-Beardsley, & Berliner, 2004; Goldhaber & Anthony, 2005; Smith, Gordon, Colby, & Wang, 2005; Sanders, Ashton, & Wright, 2005; cited in Chung, 2008, p. 1)

Based on a review of these three kinds of TPA studies, PACT researchers found evidence that preservice teachers separate practice in real classroom settings from activities and exercises in teacher preparation programs. Experts believed the evidence on preservice teachers needed to be more clearly defined, addressed, and strengthened. The impact of performance assessment on preservice teachers and preparation programs indicated a need for greater study and reporting as well. The PACT consortium wanted a TPA that was both an authentic representation of preservice teacher practice and a useful instrument in reflecting on goals, values, and practices in teacher preparation programs (Pecheone & Chung, 2006; Chung, 2008).

The PACT consortium looked at Schon's (1983) work on the concept of "reflection in action," with its application to the teacher as a reflective practitioner and Shulman's (1987) concept of teaching as "pedagogical reasoning and action," going beyond best practices to examine underlying elements of teaching. The consortium also examined the work of Baxter, Glaser, and Raghavan, 1993; Darling-Hammond, Ancess, and Falk, 1995; and Wiggins, 1998 (cited in Chung, 2008, p. 1), on using K–12 performance assessments to promote student learning and higher-order thinking.

Situated knowledge theory (Bruner, 1996; Greeno, Collins, & Resnick, 1996; cited in Chung, 2008, p. 1) and **social constructivist theory** (Gage & Berliner, 1998; Lave, 1988; Lave & Wenger, 1991; cited in Chung, 2008, p. 1), state that the teaching contexts in which teachers learn to teach may affect the extent to which their instructional practices can have an impact on learners. These learning theories were also considered by PACT researchers in informing performance assessment (Chung, 2008, p. 1).

Researchers examined the studies of novice teachers and their practicum experiences (Feiman-Nemser & Buchmann, 1983; Goodlad, 1990; Zeichner, 1992; cited in Chung, 2008, p. 1). These studies found that beginning teachers' social conditions influence what they learn from their experiences. Researchers reviewed the early work of Vygotsky (1962, 1978) on the **Zone of Proximal Development (ZPD),** in which the presence of an "other" in social interaction and communication helps push learners to the next level of learning. Tharp and Gallimore's (1988) research further applies the principle of the ZPD to teaching as assisted performance, stating that becoming a teacher requires support provided by cooperating teachers and university supervisors (cited in Chung, 2008, p.1).

The PACT developers recognized the work of the 37-state consortium of state education agencies and national education organizations known as INTASC, or the Interstate New Teacher Assessment and Support Consortium. This multistate consortium was created in 1987 and is housed at the Council of Chief State School Officers (CCSSO) in Washington, D.C. The CCSSO's "work is guided by one basic premise: An effective teacher must be able to integrate content knowledge with the specific strengths and needs of students to assure that *all* students learn and perform at high levels" (www.ccsso.org/ [Council of Chief State School Officers, 2008, p. 1]).

Because some states now offer monetary incentives for teachers to achieve National Board certification from the National Board for Professional Teaching Standards (NBPTS), the PACT consortium considered the impact of this type of certification on teacher performance assessment.

From 1987 to 1990, the Stanford Teacher Assessment Project, known as TAP, actually piloted the performance-based assessments that became the basis for NBPTS assessments. These assessments provided evidence that portfolio assessment and related activities could measure differences in skills between novices and seasoned teachers, in regard to teacher performance quality (Pecheone, 2005).

The National Board's motto of "Better Teaching, Better Learning, Better Schools" reflects its emphasis on documented evidence of teacher performance to improve pupil achievement and schools. Over 74,000 teachers have received National Board certification since 1987. Teachers who achieve the NBPTS certification in any of the 25 subject areas offered "must meet rigorous standards through intensive study, expert evaluation, self-assessment and peer review" (http://www.nbpts.org/, 2008, p. 1). A congressionally mandated study on National Board certification has been recognized by the National Research Council as positively impacting student achievement, teacher retention, and professional development.

Clinical Education

The PACT consortium noted clinical education practices as well—for example, the pivotal work of Florida's teacher education requirements. In Florida, nationally certified teachers, even those with National Board certification, are not necessarily clinical education certified, which is a requirement for licensure purposes. For teacher educators, Florida's clinical education (CE) training provides another example of a field-tested model of teacher performance assessment. Clinical education, which has been required for Florida teacher certification since the early 1990s, refers to four training modules in clinical skills that prepare classroom teachers to provide support and guidance to developing teachers and mid-career entrants (www.fldoe.org/profdev/clined.asp [Florida Department of Education, 2005]).

Clinical education put a totally new spin on teacher performance assessment, including such areas as how many males versus female pupils speak in a classroom, the teacher's physical location and movements during the lesson, and how many and what types of questions are asked by the teacher and the learners. Clinical education provides specific, detailed observations based on what is actually happening in a classroom, literally moment by moment. Clinical educators learn techniques, skills, and questions to help "focus on the Sunshine State Standards, student learning and achievement, curricular alignment, and other school improvement areas" (http://www.fldoe.org/profdev/clined.asp [Florida Department of Education, 2005, p. 1]). These observations inform the teaching process, so that practitioners can have a clearer picture of what they are doing well in the classroom, and which areas need improvement or modification. As a result, the outcomes of the Florida CE project add to the body of work on teacher performance assessment.

Teacher Education Programs

Researchers also examined several studies on teacher performance assessment in teacher education programs (Anderson & DeMeulle, 1998; Darling-Hammond & Macdonald, 2000; Darling-Hammond & Snyder, 2000; Davis & Honan, 1998; Lyons, 1996, 1998a, 1998b, 1999; Shulman, 1992; Stone, 1998; Whitford, Ruscoe, & Fickel, 2000; cited in Pecheone, 2005, p. 167). Because so many teacher preparation programs had developed successful portfolio assessments since the 1980s, researchers were especially interested in how these assessments might inform the practices of preservice teachers.

For example, Connecticut was the first state to require teacher candidates to complete portfolio assessments for the purposes of licensure. Studies of the Connecticut performance assessment have been limited and more are forthcoming, but initial findings reveal that most teachers found portfolios to be a valuable opportunity for reflection and professional growth (Pecheone, 2005).

Another teacher preparation program that informed the PACT process, Alverno College in Milwaukee, has successfully used performance assessments for two decades. Alverno's portfolio assessment system incorporates an exhibition process that includes candidates' essays, position papers, case studies, teacher performance videos, curriculum materials, and related artifacts, embedded in coursework. Studies of Alverno's program indicate that principals rate graduates as strong in the five professional educational abilities of Alverno's program, i.e., conceptualization, diagnosis, coordination, communication, and integrative interaction, although principals' ratings have some times been criticized for being unreliable and lacking variability (Pecheone, 2005).

A 1987 study by Richert conducted with teacher candidates in the Stanford Teacher Education Program also informed the PACT research process, as the researchers weighed available methods and results in teacher performance assessment. This study indicated that portfolios helped guide teachers' reflections on the content of their lessons, while peer review assisted teachers with their choice of pedagogical strategies. Richert's work, while not using portfolios directly for assessment, highlighted the potential use of portfolios, both as learning and reflection tools for preservice teachers (Pecheone, 2005).

Portfolio Assessment

Experts on the PACT process examined the portfolio assessment system of the University of Southern Maine (USM), an assessment that was first administered in 1994. The university's portfolio assessment requires candidates to select evidence of teacher performance and defend it in an interview in front of a panel of school and university faculty. A longitudinal study of the USM program indicates that (1) candidates' initial reflections are simplistic and become more elaborate over time; (2) panel questions about the candidate's portfolio choices raise the candidate's consciousness about his or her own teaching practices; (3) important aspects of teaching practice, such as teaching philosophy, are recognized and made apparent; and (4) the process of public, collaborative inquiry results in increased levels of self-awareness, in relation to teaching and learning. Both the USM portfolio system and candidates' descriptions on their views of teaching practice and pedagogical choices captured the attention of the PACT researchers (Pecheone, 2005).

California's mandated new-teacher induction program, Beginning Teacher Support and Assessment (BTSA), funded through local education agencies and varying across the state, provided PACT experts an additional insight into California's own experimentation with teacher performance assessment. Since 1996, annual surveys of administrators, beginning teachers, and their mentors (known as support providers) indicate that the participants consider BTSA systems to be fair, accurate, and helpful to professional growth and development of new teachers. Studies of the BTSA program further highlighted key differences in school cultures and varying levels of new teacher support at school sites (Pecheone, 2005).

Some BTSA programs implemented the California Formative Assessment and Support System for Teachers (CFASST), first piloted in 1998–99 to support new teachers, whereas others have developed their own performance assessments. Although findings reveal that some teachers criticize CFASST events as a "forced reflection," most understand—and welcome—the value of reflection on teaching and learning practices (Pecheone, 2005).

Another study on portfolio assessment that informed the PACT development process is the use of portfolio assessment in the fifth-year, postbaccalaureate program at the University of California at Santa Barbara (UCSB). The UCSB program requires all teacher candidates to submit a credential portfolio demonstrating their successful attainment of California teacher credentialing standards. All Masters of Education candidates at UCSB must submit a second portfolio based on evidence of reflection on individual practice and learning from teaching. Candidate follow-up studies revealed that the two types of portfolios successfully "elicited reflection in student teachers when the evidence was collected from multiple sources over time" (Pecheone, 2005, p. 168) but provided no observations of teachers in actual classroom practice.

The preservice teacher education program at California State University, Fresno, provided PACT developers with information on two groups of preservice teachers' responses to a pilot portfolio assessment (Stone, 1998; cited in Pecheone, 2005). The Fresno State study examined the effects of portfolio development on student learning and reflection. In this study, two teacher candidate groups had different levels of guidance in portfolio preparation and construction guidance. Results for the two groups show that preservice teachers benefit from mentorship and guidance in reflection, with regard to portfolio building. The Fresno State findings suggest that a supportive, collegial environment in preservice teacher preparation programs, student teaching placements, and first teaching assignments contributes to positive outcomes in promoting reflection in teacher candidates (Pecheone, 2005).

● The Impact of PACT

How PACT Addresses Research Gaps

Experts on the PACT process found a major weakness in the studies on the effects of performance assessment on preservice teachers: Such studies do not fully take into account the multiple sources and modalities of learning in *preservice experiences.* Preservice teachers have a wide range of opportunities to learn about pedagogy and teaching practice from university coursework, course assignments and assessments, school observations, student teaching experiences, and advice from cooperating teachers and university supervisors. Although these opportunities are primarily beneficial and instructive, it has been "methodogically difficult to disentangle the learning that teachers gain through performance assessments from other sources of learning" (Pecheone, 2005, p. 168). As a result, candidates' self-reports on their teaching and learning have typically relied on their own subjective judgment about what they have learned.

How PACT Addresses Assessment Gaps

The PACT Teaching Event addresses this weakness in preservice teacher assessment by assessing the key, or pillar, tasks identified by teacher education experts as essential to quality teacher performance—that is, **Planning, Instruction, Assessment, and Reflection.** Additional attention is paid to **Context** (demographics and learner needs) and **Academic Language** (language demands placed on learners at school across subjects and grade levels).

Artifacts, commentaries, and video clips of teacher candidate performance in the PACT Teaching Event provide textual evidence of teaching performance and do not sit in silos as isolated, evidentiary pieces of teaching practice, as they might in traditional portfolios or course assignments. In contrast to traditional assessments, the Teaching Event items are connected through *integration of tasks in a unified learning segment,* with deep, structured, documented analysis of pedagogical choices and learner outcomes (http://pacttpa.org [PACT, 2008]).

How PACT Addresses Other Assessment Issues

The PACT Teaching Event also addresses the weak relationship demonstrated between traditional teacher licensing tests and teacher effectiveness (Strauss & Sawyer, 1986; Ferguson, 1991, 1998; Ferguson & Ladd, 1996; National Research Council, 2001; Clotfelter, Ladd, & Vigdor, 2007; Goldhaber, 2005, 2006; cited in Pecheone, 2008, p. 1) with effect sizes for teacher licensing tests quite small (.01, .06) in recent value-added research (Pecheone, 2008, p. 1). In response to this research, the PACT consortium strived to develop an effective teacher performance assessment that focused on teachers, subjects, preparation, support, authenticity, and integration of practice with strong and significant results (Pecheone, 2008).

● Research on PACT as a Valid, Reliable Instrument of Teacher Performance Assessment

Any teacher performance assessment in California must adhere to the California Teaching Performance Assessment Design Standards, adopted by the California Teacher Credentialing Commission in December 2006. Teacher preparation programs that request alternatives to the state, or CalTPA, must meet Assessment Standard 1, with an assessment designed for validity and fairness, and Assessment Standard 2, through an assessment designed for reliability and fairness.

In order to meet Assessment Standard 1, *validity and fairness,* teacher preparation programs must meet key components for the alternative assessment:

1. Complex pedagogical assessment tasks to prompt aspects of candidate performance that measure the TPEs, with each task substantively related to two or more major domains of the TPEs, and collectively, the assessment addressing all six domains of the TPEs
2. Analysis of the assessment tasks and scoring scales to ensure that they yield important evidence that represents candidate knowledge and skill related to the TPEs, serving as a basis for determining entry-level pedagogical competence to teach the curriculum and student population of California's K–12 public schools, recording the basis and results of each analysis, and modifying the tasks and scales as needed

3. Defined scoring scales, so different candidates for credentials can earn acceptable scores on the Teaching Performance Assessment with the use of different pedagogical practices that support implementation of the K–12 content standards and curriculum frameworks

4. Development of scoring scales and assessor training procedures that focus primarily on teaching performance and minimize the effects of candidate factors that are not clearly related to pedagogical competence, such as personal attire, appearance, demeanor, speech patterns, and accents that are not likely to affect student learning

5. Clear, published statement of the intended uses of the assessment, which emphasizes the high-stakes implications of the assessment for candidates, the public schools, and K–12 students

6. Content review and editing procedures to ensure that pedagogical assessment tasks and directions to candidates are culturally and linguistically sensitive, fair, and appropriate for candidates from diverse backgrounds

7. Basic psychometric analyses to identify pedagogical assessment tasks and/or scoring scales that show differential effects in relation to candidates' race, ethnicity, language, gender, or disability, with periodic assessments and modifications to maximize the fairness of the assessment

8. Administrative accommodations that preserve assessment validity while addressing issues of access for candidates with disabilities

9. Inclusion of reflections and professional judgments of teachers, teacher supervisors, support providers of new teachers, and other preparers of teachers, regarding necessary and acceptable levels of proficiency on the part of entry-level teachers (Jacobson, 2006, p. 1)

To meet Assessment Standard 2, *reliability and fairness,* teacher preparation programs that develop alternatives to the state assessment must include these components:

1. Evidence of candidate performance through thorough field-testing of pedagogical tasks, scoring scales, and directions to candidates

2. Extensive field-testing and reporting of results of pedagogical assessment tasks and scoring scales, before the scales are used operationally in the teaching performance assessment

3. Comprehensive program to train assessors who will score candidate responses to the pedagogical assessment tasks, including task-based scoring trials

4. Periodic evaluations of the assessor training program, which include systematic feedback from assessors and assessment trainers and lead to substantive improvements in the training as needed

5. Successive administrations of the assessment to ensure consistency in elements that contribute to the reliability of scores and the accurate determination of each candidate's passing status

6. Equivalent scoring across successive administrations of the assessment and between the Commission's model and local assessments, ensured by using benchmark performances to facilitate the training of first-time assessors and continuing assessors, monitoring and recalibrating local scoring, and periodically studying proficiency levels reflected in the adopted passing standard

7. Investigation and documentation of the consistency of scores among and across assessors and across successive administrations of the assessment, with particular focus on the reliability of scores at and near the adopted passing standard

8. Appeal procedure for candidates who do not pass the assessment, including an equitable process for rescoring of evidence already submitted by an appellant candidate in the program (Jacobson, 2006, pp. 1–2)

What Sets PACT Apart from Other Assessments

The PACT Teaching Event meets California standards for alternative assessments and includes "multiple sources of data (teacher plans, teacher artifacts, student work samples, video clips of teaching, and personal reflections and commentaries) that are organized on four categories of teaching: planning, instruction, assessment, and reflection" (Pecheone & Chung, 2006, p. 1).

Unlike the National Board for Professional Teaching Standards assessments, the Teaching Event "tasks are more integrated (capturing a unified learning segment), are designed to *measure teacher performance at the preservice level* [emphasis added], and have no assessment center components. Moreover, the PACT assessment system also uses a multiple measures approach to assessing teacher competence through the use of course-embedded signature assessments" (Pecheone & Chung, 2006, p. 1).

● Piloting PACT

The first pilot of PACT occurred in 2002–03, when 395 Teaching Events were scored at regional scoring sites, with 163, or about 41 percent, double scored to evaluate interrater reliability. During the next pilot of PACT in 2003–04, 628 TEs were scored at local campuses. Of those TEs, 203, or about 32 percent, were audited through independent scoring at a PACT-sponsored, centralized audit site using experienced scorers. In both pilot years, "candidates scored significantly higher on the planning rubrics than on the other tasks and significantly lower on the academic language task" (Pecheone & Chung, 2006, p. 1).

Essential to the PACT consortium in meeting state alternative assessment standards was the ability to demonstrate the validity (content, construct, concurrent, and criterion), score reliability and consistency, bias and fairness review, and learning consequences for the PACT Teaching Event and scoring process. In order to address these key issues, the consortium considered critical questions, such as:

1. Does the TE measure what it purports to measure?
2. How well does the content of the assessments represent a particular domain of professional knowledge or skills?
3. Are PACT scores meaningful in terms of psychological or pedagogical constructs that underlie the assessment?
4. What is the relationship of the PACT scores to other indicators of candidates' competence, an area that is rarely explored in teacher licensure studies?
5. To what extent do supervisors and faculty members familiar with candidates agree with the scores candidates received on the subject-specific rubrics used in scoring the TE?
6. Are scores on the TE reliable and consistent, with interrater reliability between and among trained scorers?
7. Do the TE handbooks and rubrics used in each certification area contain any offensive or potentially offensive language and or any areas of

bias relating to race, gender, ethnicity, or cultural-linguistic background?

8. Do candidates perform differentially and significantly, with respect to specific demographic characteristics, such as the number of English learners in the student teaching placement, candidates of different ethnicities, or candidates whose primary language is English versus another language? (Pecheone & Chung, 2006)

Testing the Validity of PACT

To test the utility and validity of the PACT Teaching Event within and across subject areas, the 2003–04 assessment was piloted in 11 PACT-aligned institutions during 2003 and 13 in 2004. Varying numbers of piloting candidates were included, based on program size. Results showed that scores on the planning task were higher than scores on other tasks. The differences in scores for instruction, assessment, and reflection tasks on the PACT TE were not as pronounced as they were in a 2002–03 pilot, nor were they statistically significant (Pecheone & Chung, 2006).

A comparison of candidates' responses on a Teacher Reflection Survey, conducted by PACT during the first two years of the pilot phase, indicated that:

> Candidates in the second-year pilot were much more likely to agree that their teacher preparation program and student teaching experiences had prepared them to complete the TE (62% agreed that their program courses had prepared them in 2003 and 84% agreed in 2004; 63% agreed that their student teaching placements had prepared them in 2003 and 90% agreed in 2004). Candidates were also more likely to rate their university professors' support higher in the 2nd pilot year (42%) than they did in the 1st pilot year (28%), whereas their ratings of support received from other credential candidates, university supervisors, and cooperating teachers remained about the same or slightly declined. (Pecheone & Chung, 2006, p. 1)

Using a Spearman-Brown reliability estimate and a sample size of 2,580 scores on the PACT Teaching Event, PACT researchers found an interreliability estimate of .88, a significant result that indicated that most trained scorers gave either adjacent or the same scores on the TE. Of the trained PACT scorers, 46 percent gave an exact match on the scores they chose, 44 percent gave an adjacent score of ±1, and 10 percent had scores of ±2, with the most frequently occurring scores from 2003 to 2005 at a level 2 or level 3, both in the passing range (Pecheone, 2008).

How Experts Responded to Initial PACT Research

The PACT consortium was responsive to concerns about learning consequences, expressed in pilot-phase surveys of program directors and teacher educators within consortium campuses. In these studies, many participating campuses noted first that candidates had weaker performances on the assessment and reflection tasks of the TE. Later, programs noted that candidates were challenged in understanding and applying academic language. As a result, the consortium made efforts to provide more support and guidance in completing these specific tasks in the Teaching Event. They also included more state training for program participants, posting helpful handbooks and documents online at http://pacttpa.org (Pecheone, 2008).

In addition, survey responses from PACT-aligned institutions on learning consequences indicated that changes in curriculum and organization have been made in teacher preparation programs, as a direct consequence of participating in the PACT pilot. Of 527 pilot candidates surveyed, 70 percent reported that they were well-supported in their programs. Some 85 percent of those who reported being well-prepared by coursework and student teaching placements believed the TE assessed important aspects of their teaching knowledge and skill (Pecheone & Chung, 2006).

Summary

Teacher performance assessment continues to capture the interest of national education experts. Overall, the PACT Teaching Event holds up well to statistical analysis and scrutiny by researchers as a valid and reliable teacher performance assessment. PACT has not been without its critics and controversy, including concerns about the time and monetary costs of implementing and scoring the Teaching Event. Despite these concerns, after July 1, 2008, all candidates in multiple-subject and single-subject teacher preparation programs must receive a passing score on their state-approved assessment as part of the credential requirements. With 32 PACT-aligned public and private institutions and 29.2 percent of teacher candidates now participating, including some of the largest teacher credentialing programs such as California State University, Northridge, an increasing number of candidates in California will complete the PACT Teaching Event.

References

Chung, R. (2008). Beyond assessment: Performance assessments in teacher education. *Teacher Education Quarterly,* January 1, 2008. Retrieved January 2, 2009, from www .accessmylibrary.com/coms2/summary_0286-35679687_ITM.

Council of Chief State School Officers (CCSSO). (2008). *Strategic initiatives.* Retrieved January 2, 2009, from www.ccsso.org/.

Florida Department of Education. (2005). *Clinical educator training program overview.* Retrieved November 1, 2007, from www.fldoe.org/profdev/clined.asp.

Jacobson, P. (2006). *California teaching performance assessment design standards from the CCTC.* Retrieved October 9, 2007, from www.pacttpa.org/_files/Publications_and_ Presentations/PACT_Technical_Report_March07.pdf.

National Board for Professional Teaching. (2008). *Standards.* Retrieved January 5, 2008, from http://www.nbpts.org.

No Child Left Behind, U. S. Department of Education. (2008a). *NCLB policy.* Retrieved January 5, 2008, from www.ed.gov/nclb/landing.jhtml.

No Child Left Behind, U.S. Department of Education. (2008b). *A toolkit for teachers.* Retrieved January 3, 2008, from www.ed.gov/teachers/nclbguide/nclb-teachers-toolkit .pdf.

PACT. (2008). PACT consortium website. Retrieved January 6, 2009, from http://pacttpa .org.

Pecheone, R. (2008). *The thinking behind PACT: Performance assessment for California teachers.* Retrieved January 6, 2008, from http://pacttpa.org/_files/Publications_and_ Presentations/PACT.ppt.

Pecheone, R. (2007). *The evolution and future of statewide collaborations in studying and assessing teaching quality.* Retrieved July 8, 2009, from http://tqi.uwsa.edu/events/2007/ RayPecheoneQM2007.ppt.

Pecheone, R. (2005). *Overview of elementary literacy teaching event.* Retrieved May 11, 2007, from www.pacttpa.org/_files/Publications_and_Presentations/Appendixes_A-D.pdf.

Pecheone, R., and Chung, R. (2006). Evidence in teacher education: The Performance Assessment for California Teachers (PACT). *Journal of Teacher Education 57,* 22–36. Retrieved June 11, 2007, from http://pacttpa.org/_files/Publications_and_Presentations/PACT_Evidence_Teacher_Ed_JTE.pdf.

Schon, D. (1983). *The reflective practitioner: How professionals think in action.* London: Temple Smith.

Shulman, L. (1987). Knowledge and teaching: Foundations of the new reform. *Harvard Educational Review 57,* (1): 1–22.

Stansbury, K. (2008). English language arts teaching event candidate handbook 2008–09. Paper presented at PACT Consortium Conference, University of California at Santa Barbara, November 13.

Vygotsky, L. S. (1978). Interaction between learning and development. In M. Cole (Trans.), *Mind in Society* (pp. 79–91). Cambridge, MA: Harvard University Press.

Vygotsky, L. S. (1962). *Thought and language.* Cambridge, MA: MIT Press.

CHAPTER 1

Defining PACT

PACT is the **Performance Assessment for California Teachers.** Effective July 1, 2008, the California legislature required all elementary and secondary student teachers to pass a structured and standardized assessment of how they perform with their K–12 students. This standardized assessment known as a **CalTPA,** or California Teaching Performance Assessment, is based on a set of standards known as the **Teaching Performance Expectations (TPEs).** The PACT is an alternate TPA that has currently been adopted by 32 state and private universities and colleges in California, all of whom have teacher preparation programs.

The PACT product is essentially a structured **Teaching Event (TE),** on average a 45- to 50-page document with two 10-minute video clips that represent three to five hours or approximately one week of student teaching, known as a unified learning segment. Video clip requirements vary according to single or multiple subject and subject area; for example, elementary math candidates prepare one 15-minute video clip.

The PACT Teaching Event reflects the teacher candidate's knowledge, skills, and abilities in four key areas or tasks: **planning, instruction, assessment, and reflection.** Teacher candidates are also required to provide a **context commentary** on the demographics of their school site and target population. Additionally, they must identify and address the **academic language** needs of learners across all tasks. For a snapshot of the PACT Teaching Event structure, examine Table 2.1 on page 40.

Teaching Event Handbooks and requirement templates, rubrics and guidelines, research and benchmark samples are all shared with candidates by their teacher preparation programs. These resources aid in the preparation and successful completion of the tasks. The PACT consortium at Stanford University maintains a website with helpful handbooks, resources, research, links, and materials at http://pacttpa.org (PACT, 2008c).

How PACT was Developed

Twelve institutions of higher learning—Stanford University, San Jose State University, San Diego State University, Mills College, and eight of the nine University of California institutions—formed the original **PACT consortium** in 2001 (http://pacttpa.org [PACT, 2008c]).

Given the large number of teachers in California and the demands of NCLB, teacher performance assessment has become an increasingly critical issue for school districts and teacher preparation programs. In 2006–07, California had more than 308,000 public school teachers and a need for about 21,000 more in 2007–08. Almost all teachers, 95 percent, had the appropriate credentials in 2006, compared to 94.2 percent in 2005. About 4.8 percent of teachers were on emergency permits or waivers, and another 3.7 percent were on-the-job interns working toward their teaching credential (www.eddata.k12.ca.us/Articles/Article.asp?title=Teachers%20in%20California [Ed-Data, 2008]).

In 2001, the 12 institutions worked together to design, pilot, and evaluate an alternative assessment known as PACT, consisting of a common standardized assessment along with a set of other assessments, varying according to program. Through foundation support, a central design team established at Stanford University worked in collaboration with subject-specific development teams of faculty and student teaching supervisors from PACT member institutions (www.pacttpa.org/_files/Main/Brief_Overview_of_PACT.doc [PACT, 2008a]).

The mission of the original PACT consortium was to develop Teaching Events for piloting in the 2002–03 academic year. They solicited feedback and suggestions for improvement from faculty, supervisors, trainers, and scorers. Results from the first year were used to direct revisions for the 2003–04 academic year. The practice of using the PACT TE as a dynamic assessment was established, with an emphasis on responding to demonstrated need for teacher performance improvement identified in real class-room settings (www.pacttpa.org/_files/Main/Brief_Overview_of_PACT .doc [PACT, 2008a]).

In 2003, PACT emerged in its current form and was carefully piloted and assessed. In October 2007, **The California Commission on Teacher Credentialing (CCTC)** approved the Performance Assessment for California Teachers, and the original consortium eventually expanded to its current membership of 32 PACT-aligned institutions.

● Origins of the PACT Teaching Event

In 2001, California Senate Bill 2042 required all preservice teachers to pass a state-approved assessment to receive a preliminary teaching credential. In response to the legislative mandate, the PACT consortium of 12 California institutions with teacher preparation programs designed and piloted the performance-based assessment in 2003. This assessment came to be known as PACT, the Performance Assessment for California Teachers, with its centerpiece, the Teaching Event:

> The purpose of the Teaching Event is twofold . . . for preservice teachers, the Teaching Event focuses their attention on examining their teacher practice . . . for teacher education programs, the Teaching Event provides data that illuminates program strengths and weaknesses, which can be analyzed for program improvement (Nagle, 2006, p. 1).

The use of PACT was further strengthened on July 1, 2008, when the California legislature required all elementary and secondary student teachers to pass a structured and standardized assessment of how they perform with their K–12 students. As previously discussed, this standardized assessment was the Teaching Performance Assessment (TPA), based on a set of standards known as the Teaching Performance Expectations (TPEs). The PACT is an alternate TPA that has currently been adopted by 32 state and private universities and colleges in California, all of whom have teacher preparation programs. Some 29.2 percent of California teacher candidates complete the PACT in their individual programs (www.ctc.ca.gov/ [California Commission on Teacher Credentialing, 2008]; http://pacttpa.org [PACT, 2008c]; Pecheone, 2008).

Selecting the Teaching Event as the PACT Centerpiece

California's Commission on Teacher Credentialing presented its TPA to educators statewide in 2001, created in conjunction with the Educational Testing Service. The original CCTC teacher performance assessment, or CalTPA, basically consisted of four tasks embedded as assignments in teacher preparation program coursework. The four tasks were separate and discrete, yet teacher preparation programs desired an integrated view of teacher candidate performance that brought tasks together in a meaningful context. Many educators expressed dissatisfaction with the generic and cumbersome form, function, and features of the selected tasks in the CalTPA (Pecheone & Chung, 2006).

Teacher preparation programs expressed interest in a teacher performance assessment that would reach beyond "one-size-fits-all" paper-and-pencil artifacts and portfolios. Credentialing programs wanted to capture authentically and efficiently their teacher candidates' performance, both through documented evidence and video clips, with appropriate templates, tasks, student work samples, and rubrics.

Meeting the needs of diverse learners and subject-specific pedagogy were also essential threads in the development of the teacher performance assessment. Starting in summer 2002, the PACT consortium worked in an ongoing process to develop and pilot an integrated set of subject-specific assessments of teaching knowledge and skills aligned with the California Teaching Performance Expectations (Pecheone & Chung, 2006).

Portfolio assessments from National Board for Professional Teaching Standards, Connecticut State Department of Education, and the Interstate New Teacher Assessment and Support Consortium (INTASC) all provided models of teacher performance assessment, based on rigorous research and successful field testing. Drawing on the best features and practices of the state and national models, the PACT consortium developed a common assessment—a portfolio assessment with integrated tasks (http://pacttpa .org [PACT, 2008c]).

Construction and Scoring of the PACT Teaching Event

The Teaching Event's focus on student learning is designed to demonstrate how a candidate's practice meets the Teaching Performance Expectations (http://pacttpa.org [PACT, 2008c]). More details on the Teaching Event, the scoring process, and the rubrics can be found in Chapters 2 and 4.

● What PACT Measures

As an alternative Teacher Performance Assessment, the standardized assessment of the PACT answers six key questions related to the teacher candidate's performance in preservice or student teaching, based on the Teaching Performance Expectations and evaluated by rubrics:

1. Can the student teacher **provide a context** for the lesson that describes the demographics of and any pertinent information related to the specific target population and needs of learners?
2. Can the student teacher **plan** lessons that are developmentally appropriate and pedagogically sound, meeting the needs of English learners, diverse learners, and learners with challenges?
3. Can the student teacher **instruct** effectively, using a range of developmentally appropriate strategies that are related to stated standards, objectives, and outcomes?
4. Can the student teacher **assess** pupil learning and achievement, using appropriate formal and/or informal assessments to determine that pupils have achieved the stated objectives of the lesson?
5. Can the student teacher **reflect** clearly on the process of teaching and learning, examining the strengths and weaknesses of strategies and assessments, to improve teaching and learning and to guide the next steps?
6. Can the student teacher successfully **identify and address academic language** needs of learners throughout the lesson and assessments? (http://pacttpa.org [PACT, 2008c])

How PACT Data Are Used

In addition to providing evidence of teacher performance assessment, the data from the implementation of PACT can be used as an educative assessment in several key areas: (1) to move from compliance to inquiry; (2) to stimulate robust faculty and program conversations about candidate work samples and outcomes to inform program improvement; and (3) to make sense of the tasks, policies, and rubrics for the purposes of growth, collaboration, identity, and adopting an inquiry stance (Sloan, 2008). More information on the PACT Teaching Event, scoring, rubrics, and uses of data and evidence is discussed in Chapter 2 and Chapter 4.

Research That Supports the PACT Design

The key features of PACT are based on the "application of subject-specific pedagogical knowledge that research finds to be associated with successful teaching," specifically the work of Bransford, Brown, and Cocking (1999); Darling-Hammond (1998); Fennema et al. (1996); Grossman (1990); Porter (1988); and Shulman (1987) (cited in Pecheone & Chung, 2006, p. 23). This same body of work on teacher education challenges teacher preparation programs to provide teacher performance assessment that is authentic, is rigorous but reasonable, and indicates predictive validity (Pecheone & Chung, 2006).

In contrast to the National Board for Professional Teaching Standards assessment, which principally measures teacher performance of on-the-job teachers, the PACT assesses the teacher performance of preservice teachers or student teachers (www.nbpts.org [National Board for Professional Teaching Standards, 2009]; http://pacttpa.org [PACT, 2008c]). The PACT Teaching Event uses multiple measures to assess teacher competence through coursework-embedded signature assessments (Pecheone & Chung, 2006).

● Embedded Signature Assessments in PACT

Several teacher preparation programs in PACT-aligned California universities identified assignments, known as **Embedded Signature Assignments (ESAs),** that they believed were essential to their specific program values and teacher candidate needs. For example, a university teacher credentialing program dedicated to PACT may also focus on the social environment of the classroom, specific curricular features, classroom management, or a community study.

As a result of specific program features, institutions may embed related signature assignments into one or more of their teacher candidate courses. According to PACT, "The long term goal of PACT is to add ESAs as an optional component of the complete Teaching Performance Assessment package" (http://pacttpa.org [PACT, 2008c]).

Embedded Signature Assignments reflect the local program component of PACT, in contrast to the Teaching Event, which is standardized across programs. ESAs offer teacher preparation programs an opportunity to reflect their own program emphases and values, so that programs can either develop ESAs or use the Teaching Event "as is" for their TPA.

Differences between Embedded Signature Assessments and Regular Classroom Assignments

The PACT consortium clarifies the difference between embedded signature and regular classroom assignments this way:

> The difference between ESAs and many classroom assignments is that the ESAs have more formalized scoring criteria that are used by more than one person. If they are to be used to compensate for failing scores on the Teaching Event, however, then they will need to demonstrate the same rigorous psychometric properties, e.g., inter-rater reliability. . . . Many longtime institutions in PACT have developed ESAs, including formal scoring criteria, and are piloting them and analyzing scores. (www.pacttpa.org/_main/hub .php?pageName=Embedded_Signature_Assessments_(ESAs) [PACT, 2008b, p. 1]).

Examples of Embedded Signature Assessments

Examples of ESAs are available from various teacher preparation programs. For example, the University of California at San Diego "developed a new ESA focusing on the social environment of the classroom, which collects evidence over time across several courses. . . . Some of these (e.g., curriculum unit) focus on similar areas of teaching as the Teaching Event, while others (e.g., community study) focus on areas that are not addressed in any depth in the Teaching Event" (www.pacttpa.org/_main/hub.php? pageName=Embedded_Signature_Assessments_(ESAs) [PACT, 2008b, p. 1]).

Some teacher preparation programs include classroom observations of specific elements, such as classroom management, or an in-depth case study of a learner. At a particular university and within a single course, an ESA such as a curriculum unit on social justice may be required. Embedded Signature Assessments help capture and preserve the individual flavor and nature of various teacher preparation programs in PACT-aligned institutions, while attending to the essential elements of teacher performance assessment.

California's Alternate TPAs

The California Commission on Teacher Credentialing allows accredited teacher preparation programs to use their own valid and reliable Teacher Performance Assessment (TPA) as an alternative to the CalTPA, subject to approval by the CCTC (http://www.ctc.ca.gov/reports/ab471/report.pdf [California Commission on Teacher Credentialing, 2001]). PACT is an example of an **alternate TPA,** and California State University, Fresno, won approval from the CCTC to require its teacher candidates to complete an alternate TPA known as FAST (Fresno Assessment of Student Teachers).

FAST assesses the pedagogical competence of preservice teachers and interns with regard to their successful demonstration of the TPEs. Candidates are assessed during their final student teaching placement on four tasks known as projects (i.e., a comprehensive lesson plan, a site visitation, teaching sample, and holistic proficiency). A four-point, task-specific rubric evaluates each assessment task in the FAST on multiple TPEs (www.ctc.ca.gov/commission/agendas/2008-06/2008-06-3G-insert.pdf [CCTC, 2008b]).

The California Teacher Performance Assessment

The **CalTPA** is the state-approved teacher performance assessment, but CCTC provides a process for institutions to receive approval for an alternative to the CalTPA, known as an alternate TPA (www.ctc.ca.gov [CCTC, 2001, 2008]). PACT is one such alternate TPA.

According to CCTC, the CalTPA requires candidates to complete a series of four performance tasks, increasing in complexity. All but one of the tasks are done with actual K–12 students, and the four tasks measure the TPEs in multiple ways. The CalTPA is embedded within teacher preparation programs and administered and scored by program sponsors. CalTPA performance tasks consist of subject-specific pedagogy, designing instruction, assessing learning, and culminating teaching experience (www.ctc.ca .gov/educator-prep/TPA-files/CalTPA-general-info.pdf [CCTC, 2008a]).

How the CalTPA Became Required by State Law

According to the California Commission on Teacher Credentialing, the history of the legislative mandate emerged through the following set of important events:

1. Senate Bill 2042, known as SB2042 (Chapter 548 Statutes of 1998), required all candidates for a preliminary Multiple and Single Subject Teaching Credential to pass an assessment of teaching performance in order to earn a teaching credential, designed to measure the candidate's knowledge, skills and ability with relation to California's Teaching Performance Expectations (TPEs).

2. Implementation of the TPA requirement of SB2042 was delayed by the Commission in 2003 in response to requests received from the Legislature and others during the state's fiscal crisis at that time.

3. SB1209 (Chapter 517, Statutes of 2006), however, mandated the implementation of the teaching performance assessment requirement for all multiple- and single-subject professional teacher preparation programs as of July 1, 2008. *The Commission took action in December 2006 to require that any candidate who begins a teacher preparation program on or after July 1, 2008 must pass a Teaching Performance Assessment (TPA) prior to recommendation for a credential* [emphasis added].

4. The CalTPA is the Commission TPA model. The CalTPA measures those features of the Teaching Performance Expectations (TPEs) that describe the knowledge and abilities required of beginning California teachers, adopted by the Commission in September 2001.

5. The current Commission-approved alternate models are PACT (Performance Assessment for California Teachers) and FAST (Fresno Assessment of Student Teachers) (www.ctc.ca.gov/ [CCTC, 2001, 2008]).

New Program Standards and the TPA

In its implementation of SB2042, the California Commission on Teacher Credentialing (CCTC) added five new program quality standards, describing the TPA and providing governance for its implementation. Known as *Category E: Assessment Quality Standards,* the five program quality standards govern how the TPA will be designed, implemented, and administered. Program Standards 19 to 23 specifically address the TPA criteria for "validity, reliability, accuracy, fairness, assessor qualifications and training, assessment administration, resources, and reporting procedures" (Jones, 2005, p. 3).

The CCTC specifically states that the TPA will measure each candidate's ability to assist students to meet or exceed state content and performance standards through a fair, valid, reliable teacher performance assessment that accurately assesses the TPE (http://www.ctc.ca.gov/, 2001).

As Chair of the California Commission on Teacher Credentialing and Dean of the Graduate School of Education at University of California Berkeley, P. David Pearson stated:

> I was thrilled to join my fellow commissioners in unanimously supporting PACT's implementation. This and the CA-TPA assessment put California in a position of national leadership in teacher assessment, creating a clear and consistent pathway for novice teachers to follow in their quest for real teacher quality—namely, the knowledge and skills they need to bring high quality instruction to all students. (www.srnleads.org/data/pdfs/pact_pr.pdf, 2005s [School Redesign Network Leadership, 2005, p. 1])

● How PACT and CalTPA Differ

Unlike the candidates who complete the CalTPA designed by the California Commission on Teacher Credentialing, PACT candidates are prompted by the task design to make connections among tasks. Candidates must also integrate learning strategies and outcomes, provide context and rationales for artifacts, address academic language across all tasks, and embrace depth over coverage (http://pacttpa.org, 2008). Greater *connections among tasks, depth,* and *reflection* are three key features of the PACT Teaching

Event noted by researchers as essential differences between PACT and the CalTPA (Pecheone & Chung, 2006).

California Teacher Preparation Programs That Do Not Use PACT

Universities such as California State University, San Marcos, and California State University, Los Angeles, require teacher candidates to complete the CalTPA, approved by the CCTC for credentialing. Currently, 29.2 percent of teacher credential candidates in the state are assessed through PACT (Pecheone, 2008). A regularly updated list of participating PACT universities and teacher preparation programs, both public and private, can be found at the PACT website, http://pacttpa.org (PACT, 2008c).

● How Multiple-Subject (Elementary) and Single-Subject (Secondary) Frameworks Differ in PACT

The design of the PACT framework is consistent across all subject areas, with separate handbooks available for each of 14 specific subject areas in secondary education. Multiple-subject (elementary) PACT differs in that multiple-subject candidates (1) choose either literacy or numeracy as their overarching focus for the Teaching Event; and then (2) address context, planning, implementing instruction, assessment, and reflection, in two of four tasks selected from literacy, mathematics, history/social science, and science; and (3) may prepare one 15-minute video clip instead of the two that single-subject candidates prepare.

Single-subject candidates complete their PACT Teaching Event in one of 14 areas that represents their teaching field. For the 14 subject areas that currently have single-subject PACT Teaching Event Handbooks available (includes the four bilingual single-subject handbooks), examine Figure 1.1.

Regardless of the area of specialization, multiple or single subject, or teaching content area, such as English language arts or mathematics, all candidates must demonstrate knowledge of the Teaching Performance Expectations (TPEs) in the PACT Teaching Event.

FIGURE **1.1**

Single-Subject Areas with PACT Teaching Event Handbooks

1. Agriculture (General)
2. Agriculture (Science Emphasis)
3. Agriculture (Technology and Design)
4. Art
5. English Language Arts (and Bilingual English Language Arts)
6. Health science
7. History/social science (and Bilingual History-Social Science)
8. Home economics
9. Industrial technology
10. Mathematics (and Bilingual Mathematics)
11. Music
12. Physical education
13. Science (and Bilingual Science)
14. World language

Source: http://pacttpa.org (2008c).

The Teaching Performance Expectations

The **Teaching Performance Expectations (TPEs)** represent what teachers should know and do and provide the foundation for professional standards of performance and conduct.

The 13 California Teaching Performance Expectations, placed in six domains of the **California Standards for the Teaching Profession (CSTP)**, delineate the attributes that elementary and secondary teachers should attain to be effective educators, are found in Figure 1.2:

FIGURE **1.2**

California Teaching Performance Expectations (TPEs)

A. **Making Subject Matter Comprehensible to Students**

   TPE 1—Specific Pedagogical Skills for Subject Matter Instruction

   a. **Subject-Specific Pedagogical Skills for Multiple-Subject (Elementary) Teaching Assignments**
   Understanding the state-adopted academic content standards
   Understanding how to teach the subject matter in the standards
   Planning instruction that addresses the standards

Demonstrating the ability to teach to the standards

b. **Subject-Specific Pedagogical Skills for Single-Subject (Secondary) Teaching Assignments**

Understanding the state-adopted academic content standards

Understanding how to teach the subject matter in the standards

Planning instruction that addresses the standards

Demonstrating the ability to teach to the standards

B. **Assessing Student Learning**

TPE 2—Monitoring Student Learning During Instruction

Determining student progress toward achieving the state-adopted academic content standards

Using instructional strategies and techniques to support students' learning

TPE 3—Interpretation and Use of Assessments

Understanding a range of assessments

Using and interpreting a range of assessments

Giving feedback on assessment results

C. **Engaging and Supporting Students in Learning**

TPE 4—Making Content Accessible

Addressing state-adopted academic content standards

Prioritizing and sequencing content

Selecting and using various instructional strategies, activities, and resources to facilitate student learning

TPE 5—Student Engagement

Understanding of academic learning goals

Ensuring active and equitable participation

Monitoring student progress and extending student thinking

TPE 6—Developmentally Appropriate Teaching Practices

a. **Developmentally Appropriate Practices in Grades K–3**

Understanding important characteristics of the learners

Designing instructional activities

Providing developmentally appropriate educational experiences

b. **Developmentally Appropriate Practices in Grades 4–8**

Understanding important characteristics of the learners

Designing instructional activities

Providing developmentally appropriate educational experiences

c. **Developmentally Appropriate Practices in Grades 9–12**

Understanding important characteristics of the learners

Designing instructional activities

Providing developmentally appropriate educational experiences

(continues)

FIGURE **1.2**

California Teaching Performance Expectations (TPEs) (*continued*)

TPE 7—Teaching English Learners

Understanding and applying theories, principles, and instructional practices for English Language Development

Understanding how to adapt instructional practices to provide access to the state-adopted student content standards

Drawing upon student backgrounds and language abilities to provide differentiated instruction

---

D. Planning Instruction and Designing Learning Experiences for Students

TPE 8—Learning about Students

Understanding child and adolescent development

Understanding how to learn about students

Using methods to learn about students

Connecting student information to learning

TPE 9—Instructional Planning

Establishing academic learning goals

Connecting academic content to the students backgrounds, needs, and abilities

Selecting strategies/activities/materials/resources

E. Creating and Maintaining Effective Environments for Student Learning

TPE 10—Instructional Time

Allocating instructional time

Managing instructional time

TPE 11—Social Environment

Understanding the importance of the social environment

Establishing a positive environment for learning

Maintaining a positive environment for learning

F. Developing as a Professional Educator

TPE 12—Professional, Legal, and Ethical Obligations

Taking responsibility for student academic learning outcomes

Knowing and applying professional and ethical obligations

Knowing and applying legal obligations

TPE 13—Professional Growth

Evaluating teaching practices and subject matter knowledge

Using reflection and feedback to improve teaching practice and subject matter knowledge

---

Source: www.ctc.ca.gov/educator-prep/TPA-files/TPEs-ETS-salient.pdf, 2003.

A Quick Overview of the TPEs

An overview of key indicators of the California Teaching Performance Expectations (TPEs) can be found in Figure 1.3.

How the California TPEs Were Developed

The TPEs form the foundation of teacher knowledge, dispositions, and skills in the classroom. According to the California Commission on Teacher Credentialing, "Based on the California Standards for the Teaching Profession (CSTP), the Teaching Performance Expectations (TPEs) were developed through rigorous research and consultation with California educators by the California Commission on Teacher Credentialing (CCTC) to describe

FIGURE **1.3**

California Teaching Performance Expectations (TPEs): Quick Overview

A. Specific Pedagogical Skills for Subject Matter Instruction

TPE **1**—Specific Pedagogical Skills for Subject Matter Instruction
TPE **2**—Monitoring Student Learning During Instruction

B. Assessing Student Learning

TPE **3**—Interpretation and Use of Assessments
TPE **4**—Making Content Accessible

C. Engaging and Supporting Students in Learning

TPE **5**—Student Engagement
TPE **6**—Developmentally Appropriate Teaching Practices
TPE **7**—Teaching English Learners

D. Planning Instruction and Designing Learning Experiences for Students

TPE **8**—Learning about Students
TPE **9**—Instructional Planning

E. Creating and Maintaining Effective Environments for Student Learning

TPE **10**—Instructional Time
TPE **11**—Social Environment

F. Developing as a Professional Educator

TPE **12**—Professional, Legal, and Ethical Obligations
TPE **13**—Professional Growth

Source: Adapted from www.ctc.ca.gov/educator-prep/TPA-files/TPEs-ETS-Salient.pdf, 2003.

the set of knowledge, skills and abilities beginning teachers should be able to demonstrate" (http://www.ctc.ca.gov/ [CCTC, 2008]).

Following the legislative mandate of California Senate Bill 2042 approved in the fall of 1998, all preliminary credential candidates were required to pass a Teaching Performance Assessment. This TPA is based on a series of 13 Teacher Performance Expectations developed by the CCTC, in consultation with California educators and based on research.

Institutions Outside California Currently Using PACT

The University of Washington is currently using a form of PACT in its teacher preparation program known as the PPA (Performance-Based Pedagogy Assessment) and is engaged in rigorous research on data analysis and outcomes for the assessment (McDonald & Peck, 2008). Illinois College has also begun using PACT in its teacher preparation program (http://pacttpa.org [PACT, 2008c]).

PACT and Special Education

Currently, there is no PACT for special education, but special education teacher preparation programs across the state are considering whether, how, and when to implement PACT. There are PACT Teaching Event Handbooks in literacy and mathematics for concurrent multiple subject and education specialists (candidates who are pursuing both elementary and special education credentialing).

PACT and Bilingual Education

Bilingual Education Teaching Event Handbooks are available on the http://pacttpa.org website. Bilingual, cross-cultural, language acquisition development (BCLAD) candidates who teach in dual immersion programs—for example, in English and Spanish—may elect to write their Teaching Events in the primary language they use to teach literacy or mathematics. Thus, if a candidate teaches the subject of the Teaching Event (TE) in Spanish, the TE may be written in Spanish and scored by trained PACT scorers proficient in Spanish.

For multiple-subject (elementary) candidates, PACT Teaching Event Handbooks are available in bilingual literacy and in mathematics. For single-subject (secondary) candidates, PACT Teaching Event Handbooks are available in bilingual English language arts, history/social science, mathematics, and science (http://pacttpa.org [PACT, 2008c]).

How PACT Aligns with State Standards and Teacher Preparation Programs

A 2005 study conducted by Peter Jones of the University of California, Irvine, indicates that "the series of PACT assessment handbooks and their associated rubrics are both broadly and deeply associated with the CSTP [California Standards for the Teaching Profession] domains as well as the individual TPE" (p. 17).

In addition, Linda Darling-Hammond, Ray Pecheone, Ruth Chung, and Kendyll Stansbury of Stanford University have been persistent champions of successful efforts to demonstrate the validity and reliability of the PACT Teaching Event through the pilots of early adopter institutions and current, ongoing work of participating institutions. For the PACT TE, research findings demonstrate content validity, a bias and fairness review, construct validity, score consistency and reliability, concurrent validity, criterion validity, and significant learning consequences (Pecheone & Chung, 2006).

Essentially, the research findings on the PACT Teaching Event indicate that *the assessment measures what it says it will*—teaching performance— in a way that is accurate, free of bias, reliable over time, built on sound pedagogical or psychological constructs, consistent in outcomes, correlated to other indicators of teacher candidates' performance, and meaningful in learning consequences for the teacher candidate:

> A driving principle in the design and development of the PACT assessment was that the act of putting together a TE would significantly influence the way candidates think about and reflect on their teaching because of the design and formative nature of the assessment. This hypothesis is supported by mounting evidence. (Pecheone & Chung, 2006, p. 32)

It was also the intent of the PACT that the TE scores could be used for teacher preparation program improvement. The Teaching Event results provide useful feedback information to participating programs through a detailed snapshot of what their candidates are doing well—and areas in which they need improvement (http://pacttpa.org [PACT, 2008c]).

PACT and No Child Left Behind

The No Child Left Behind (NCLB) Act of 2001, federal legislation commonly known by its nickname "Nickelby," requires states to train and credential *highly qualified teachers* who have subject matter expertise and state certification. The NCLB mandated that local educational agencies develop a plan to ensure that all teachers assigned to teach core academic subjects meet the NCLB requirements by the 2005–06 school year (O'Connell, 2005).

The premise of NCLB is that improving teacher quality will improve educational opportunities for all children (http://www.ed.gov/nclb/landing.jhtml [No Child Left Behind, 2008]). PACT is a state-approved assessment of teacher quality and performance, focused on evidence of student learning, that aligns with NCLB's key requirements (http://pacttpa.org [PACT, 2008c]).

The three requirements for teacher compliance for California teachers under NCLB guidelines state that teachers must (1) have a bachelor's degree, (2) have a state credential or intern certificate or be currently enrolled in an approved CCTC intern program, and (3) demonstrate core subject matter competence (O'Connell, 2005, p. 5).

Additional Requirements for Teacher Licensure in California

In order to receive a preliminary teaching credential, which is valid for five years, candidates must earn a bachelor's degree, pass the California Basic Educational Skills Test (CBEST) or another approved basic skills test, demonstrate subject matter knowledge in the subject(s) they plan to teach, and participate in a state-approved teacher preparation program. For subject matter clearance, multiple-subject candidates must pass the California Subject Examination for Teachers (CSET) and the Reading Instruction Competence Assessment (RICA), while single-subject candidates must pass CSET or receive subject matter clearance from the university department of their major teaching field.

After receiving a preliminary credential, beginning teachers have five years to earn a clear teaching credential, which requires them to complete a beginning teacher induction program. National Board for Professional

Teaching Standards certification can also be used to obtain a clear credential (http://www.nbpts.org [NBPTS, 2009]). The clear credential must be renewed through professional development workshops and teacher in-service every five years (http://www.edsource.org/iss_capacity_teachers .html [Ed Source, 2008]).

● Summary

Effective July 1, 2008, all multiple-subject (elementary) and single-subject (secondary) teacher candidates in California are required to pass an assessment of their teaching performance with K–12 students. The PACT consortium designed and evaluated a successful alternative performance assessment known as the Teaching Event. The TE is based on four pillars of teaching: planning, instruction, assessment, and reflection, with attention to context (demographics and needs of diverse learners) and academic language across all tasks.

Currently, 32 public and private institutions of higher education and teacher preparation programs in California are engaged in ongoing PACT implementation and research, with 29.2 percent of candidates completing their credential through the assessment. The Performance Assessment for California Teachers has shown itself to be an authentic, reliable, valid assessment of preservice teacher performance that informs effective teacher practice and contributes to teacher preparation program improvement.

● References

California Commission on Teacher Credentialing (CCTC). (2008a). *CalTPA: California teacher performance assessment.* Retrieved January 2, 2009, from www.ctc.ca.gov/ educator-prep/TPA-files/CalTPA-general-info.pdf.

California Commission on Teacher Credentialing (CCTC). (2008b). *Recommendation for approval of the Fresno Assessment of Student Teachers (FAST).* Retrieved December 15, 2007, from www.ctc.ca.gov/commission/agendas/2008-06/2008-06-3G-insert.pdf.

California Commission on Teacher Credentialing (CCTC). (2001, 2008). Retrieved January 15, 2009, from www.ctc.ca.gov/.

Ed-Data. (2008). *State of California education profile, 2007–08.* Retrieved January 2, 2009, from www.eddata.k12.ca.us/Articles/Article.asp?title=Teachers%20in%20California.

EdSource. (2008). *Teachers in California.* Retrieved January 3, 2009, from www.edsource .org/iss_capacity_teachers.html.

Jones, P. (2005). An examination of teacher preparation: Program standard 19a requirements and the performance assessment for California teachers. In Appendix E,

Technical report of the performance assessment for California teachers, pp. 3, 17. Retrieved December 15, 2007, from www.pacttpa.org/_files/Publications_and_Presentations/PACT_Technical_Report_March07.pdf.

McDonald, M., and Peck, C. (2008). Organizational factors affecting use of PACT data for program improvement. Paper presented at PACT Consortium Conference, University of California at Santa Barbara, November 13.

Nagle, J. (2006). Performance assessment for California teachers (PACT) teaching event: Using state accountability measures of teaching to enhance critically reflective practice. Paper presented at the annual meeting of the American Association of College of Teacher Education, San Diego.

National Board for Professional Teaching Standards (NBPTS). (2009). Retrieved February 28, 2009, from www.nbpts.org.

No Child Left Behind. (2008). U.S. Department of Education. Retrieved January 6, 2009, from www.ed.gov/nclb/landing.jhtml.

O'Connell, J. (2005). *No Child Left Behind Act of 2001: Teacher requirements.* Retrieved April 10, 2007, from www.cde.ca.gov/nclb/sr/tq/documents/teacherreq05.ppt.

PACT. (2008a). *A brief overview: PACT.* Retrieved January 5, 2009, from www.pacttpa.org/_files/Main/Brief_Overview_of_PACT.doc.

PACT. (2008b). *Embedded signature assessments (ESAs).* Retrieved January 15, 2009, from www.pacttpa.org/_main/hub.php?pageName=Embedded_Signature_Assessments_(ESAs).

PACT. (2008c). PACT consortium website. Retrieved January 6, 2009, from http://pacttpa.org.

Pecheone, R. (2008). *The thinking behind PACT: Performance assessment for California teachers.* Retrieved January 6, 2009, from http://pacttpa.org/_files/Publications_and_Presentations/PACT.ppt.

Pecheone, R., and Chung, R. (2006). Evidence in teacher education: The Performance Assessment for California Teachers (PACT). *Journal of Teacher Education 57,* 22–36. Retrieved June 11, 2007, from http://pacttpa.org/_files/Publications_and_Presentations/PACT_Evidence_Teacher_Ed_JTE.pdf.

School Redesign Network Leadership, Stanford University. (2005). PACT: *State Commission approves new performance assessment for credentialing California teachers.* Retrieved March 20, 2007, from www.srnleads.org/data/pdfs/pact_pr.pdf.

Sloan, T. (2008). PACT as an educative assessment. Paper presented at annual PACT conference, University of California at Santa Barbara, November 13.

CHAPTER 2

The PACT Teaching Event

The PACT Teaching Event is, on average, a 45- to 50-page structured document with two 10-minute video clips that represents three to five hours of student teaching—approximately one week—known as a **unified learning segment.** Video clip requirements vary according to single or multiple subjects and subject area; for example, elementary math candidates create one 15-minute clip.

The PACT TE reflects the teacher candidate's knowledge, skills, and abilities in four key areas or tasks: planning, instruction, assessment, and reflection. Teacher candidates are also required to provide a **context commentary** on the demographics of their school site and specific features of their target population, as well as identify and address the **academic language** needs of learners across all tasks. For a snapshot of the PACT teaching event structure, examine Table 2.1.

The focus of the PACT Teaching Event is clearly on student learning. Teacher candidates must showcase the strategies they use to make subject matter accessible to students and support students in their learning. Candidates not only must demonstrate effective practices but also explain the thinking that underlies them, along with an analysis of the strategies used to connect student learning with content. The effects of instructional design and teaching practices, with particular attention to the needs of diverse learners, must be examined in the process of completing the PACT Teaching Event (www.sandiego.edu/soles/programs/learning_and_teaching/credential_programs/pact_teaching_event.php [PACT Teaching Event, 2008, p. 1]).

TABLE **2.1**

A Snapshot of the PACT Teaching Event Structure

Context for Learning

• Instructional Context Form
• Context for Learning Commentary

Planning	Instruction	Assessment	Reflection
Daily lesson plans	Video clips	Analysis of whole class	Daily reflections
Handouts, overheads, supplementary materials	Instruction commentary	achievement + 3 student work samples	Reflective commentary
Planning commentary		Analysis of learning for 2 of the 3 students	
		Assessment commentary	

Academic Language

(Evidence gathered across tasks)

Source: R. Pecheone, http://pacttpa.org, 2008. Used with permission.

The PACT TE is more formally described by the original design team as

> a subject-specific portfolio-based assessment of teaching performance that is completed by student teachers to demonstrate their readiness for a full-time classroom teaching assignment. It is aligned with the California Teaching Performance Expectations and the relevant California student academic content standards and/or curriculum frameworks. . . . Teaching candidates complete the Teaching Event during their teacher preparation program. (Stansbury, 2006, p. 1).

● Five Required Tasks of the Teaching Event

The Teaching Event consists of 5 tasks, with academic language identified and addressed across all tasks (www.sandiego.edu/soles/programs/learning_and_teaching/credential_programs/pact_teaching_event.php [PACT Teaching Event, 2008, p. 1]):

Task 1: Context for Learning

The Context for Learning task is a brief overview of important features of the classroom context that influence instructional decisions during the learning segment. It provides evidence of (1) candidates' knowledge of their students and (2) candidates' ability to identify and summarize important factors related to their students' learning and the school environment.

Task 2: Planning for Instruction and Assessment

The Planning for Instruction and Assessment task describes and explains candidates' plans for the learning segment. It demonstrates their ability to organize curriculum, instruction, and assessment to help their students meet the standards for the curriculum content and to develop academic language related to that content. It provides evidence of their ability to select, adapt, or design learning tasks and materials that offer their students equitable access to subject matter content.

Task 3: Instructing Students and Supporting Learning

The Instructing Students and Supporting Learning task illustrates how candidates work with their students to improve their skills and strategies in the content area during instruction. It provides evidence of their ability to engage students in meaningful tasks and monitor their understanding.

Task 4: Assessing Student Learning

The Assessing Student Learning task illustrates how candidates diagnose student learning needs through the analysis of student work samples. This task provides evidence of candidates' ability to (1) select an assessment tool and criteria that are aligned with their central focus, student standards, and learning objectives; (2) analyze student performance on an assessment in relation to student needs and the identified learning objectives; and (3) use this analysis to identify next steps in instruction for the whole class and individual students.

Task 5: Reflecting on Teaching and Learning

The Reflecting on Teaching and Learning task describes what candidates learned from teaching the learning segment. It provides evidence of their ability to analyze their teaching and their students' learning to improve teaching practice.

Quick Overviews

For a quick overview of the Teaching Event structure, see Table 2.1. For a summary of how Teaching Event requirements match the Teaching

Performance Expectations, see Table 2.2. A list and discussion of the TPEs are available in Chapter 1.

● More Information about PACT Teaching Events

Academic Language

Chapter 3 provides a definition and discussion of academic language, along with applications to the PACT Teaching Event.

Subjects Available in Multiple-Subject (Elementary) and Single-Subject (Secondary) Areas

Please examine Figure 2.1 for a list of multiple- and single-subject areas that have Teaching Event Handbooks currently available on the PACT website (http://pacttpa.org/_main/hub.php?pageName=Teaching_Event_Handbooks#Handbookshttp://pacttpa.org [2008d]).

Purpose of the Teaching Event Handbooks

The Teaching Event Handbooks available on the PACT website (http://pacttpa.org) provide (1) step-by-step guidance for teacher candidates on how to make effective choices in selecting artifacts and writing commentaries and (2) an overview and template for constructing the Teaching Event in each designated subject area. Some teacher preparation programs also make the Teaching Event Handbooks available to candidates through links on their own websites and in paper form.

Formats for Submitting the Teaching Event

Each teacher preparation program has its own policies and procedures governing the submission of the Teaching Event, but many institutions require candidates to submit their completed Teaching Event electronically, including video clips.

Electronic portfolio management systems currently in use include Taskstream (https://www.taskstream.com/pub/); LiveText (https://college.livetext.com/); Teachscape (www.teachscape.com/html/ts/nps/index.html); and local platforms specific to an institution or selected group of users, such as the G*STAR Electronic Portfolio System used at University of California Riverside (https://www.gstar.ucr.edu/gstar2006/AboutGSTAR.ppt).

TABLE **2.2**

Teaching Event Overview (Aligned with Teaching Performance Expectations)

Teaching Event Task	What to Do	What to Submit
1. Context for Learning (TPEs 7, 8)	✓ Provide relevant information about your instructional context and your students as learners.	☐ Context Form ☐ Context Commentary
2. Planning for Instruction and Assessment (TPEs 1, 2, 3, 4, 6, 7, 8, 9, 10, 12)	✓ Select an instructional segment of 3 to 5 lessons that support learning. ✓ Create an instruction and assessment plan for the learning segment and write lesson plans. ✓ Write a commentary that explains your thinking behind the plans. ✓ Record daily reflections, to submit in the reflection section of the Teaching Event.	☐ Lesson Plans for Learning Segment ☐ Instructional Materials ☐ Planning Commentary
3. Instructing Students and Supporting Learning (TPEs 1, 2, 3, 4, 5, 6, 7, 10, 11)	✓ Review your plans and prepare to videotape your class. Identify opportunities for students to use relevant skills and strategies. ✓ Videotape the lesson you have identified. ✓ Review the videotape to identify one or two video clips portraying the required features of your teaching. The total running time should not exceed 15 minutes. ✓ Write a commentary that analyzes your teaching and your students' learning in the video clip(s).	☐ Video Clip(s) ☐ Video Label Form ☐ Instruction Commentary
4. Assessing Student Learning (TPEs 2, 3, 4, 5, 13)	✓ Select one student assessment from the learning segment and analyze student work using evaluative criteria (or a rubric). ✓ Identify three student work samples that illustrate class trends in what students did and did not understand. ✓ Write a commentary that analyzes the extent to which the class met the standards/objectives, analyzes the individual learning of two students represented in the work samples, and identifies next steps in instruction.	☐ Student Work Samples ☐ Evaluative Criteria or Rubric ☐ Assessment Commentary
5. Reflecting on Teaching and Learning (TPEs 7, 8, 13)	✓ Provide your daily reflections. ✓ Write a commentary about what you learned from teaching this learning segment.	☐ Daily Reflections ☐ Reflective Commentary

Source: suse-step.stanford.edu/elementary/handbook_documents/PACT%20Teaching%20Event%20Overview.doc (Stanford University School of Education [2007], p. 1).

FIGURE 2.1

Teaching Event Handbook Subjects

Multiple-Subject (Elementary) Teaching Event Handbooks	Single-Subject (Secondary) Teaching Event Handbooks	
Elementary Literacy	Agriculture (General)	Mathematics
Elementary Mathematics	Agriculture (Science Emphasis)	Music
Bilingual Elementary Literacy		Physical Education
Bilingual Elementary Mathematics	Agriculture (Technology and Design)	Science
		World Languages
Concurrent MS/Educational Specialist—Literacy	Art	Bilingual English— Language Arts
	English Language Arts	
Concurrent MS/Educational Specialist—Mathematics	Health Science	Bilingual History— Social Science
	Home Economics	
	History/Social Science	Bilingual Mathematics
	Industrial Technology Education	Bilingual Science

Source: http://pacttpa.org (PACT, 2008a).

Samples of Completed Teaching Events

Benchmark samples of Teaching Events used by teacher preparation programs and at PACT scoring sessions are proprietary information and are not available in the public domain. However, with permission from candidates, teacher preparation programs can share samples and models within their own programs to guide the process of constructing the Teaching Event. More information on the PACT benchmark samples, rubrics, and scoring is discussed in Chapter 4.

Support Provided to Teacher Candidates in Completing the Teaching Event

Teacher preparation programs in PACT-aligned institutions provide assistance to candidates in completing the Teaching Event in a variety of ways. Designated coursework, seminars, and workshop sessions, both in-class and online, all assist candidates. Acceptable forms of support for candidates completing a Teaching Event include these:

1. Explaining the general design of curriculum materials and instructional or assessment strategies

2. Referring candidates to curriculum materials, research articles, experienced teachers, and support documents found on the PACT website (http://pacttpa.org)
3. Asking probing/clarifying questions of the candidate that encourage candidates to analyze and reflect more deeply and/or clearly on their artifacts (Stansbury, 2006, pp. 2–3)
4. Providing and discussing samples of previously completed Teaching Events
5. Pointing out relationships between learning and assessment tasks in coursework to tasks in the Teaching Event
6. Supporting candidates in creating a timeline for completion of the Teaching Event
7. Providing technical and logistical support/training for videotaping and uploading documents and video clips to electronic platforms (Stansbury, 2006, p. 1)

In addition, The PACT website provides several documents to assist candidates in completing the Teaching Event and understanding the rubrics used to score it, such as:

1. *Making Good Choices,* which answers questions about artifacts and commentaries for each Teaching Event task and explains generally how each task is scored (www.pacttpa.org/_main/hub.php?pagename= Supporting_Documents_for_Candidates [PACT, 2008c]).
2. *Selecting a Learning Segment,* which recommends that "candidates should identify a concept to teach, not a standard, . . . when selecting a learning segment for the PACT TE" (http://pacttpa.org/_main/hub.php? pagename=Supporting_Documents_for_Candidates [PACT, 2008c]).
3. *PACT Videotaping Polices* and *Procedures for Videotaping,* which provide guidance on effective videotape procedures and explain how to secure videotape permission in classrooms (www.pacttpa.org/_main/ hub.php?pageName=Supporting_Documents_for_Candidates [2008c]).
4. *Thinking Behind the Rubrics,* which explains to candidates, faculty, student teaching supervisors, and assessors the key concepts of each rubric and the distinctions between performances at adjacent levels of the rubric (Stansbury, 2006, p. 1; http://pacttpa.org [PACT, 2008a]).
5. *Teaching Event Authenticity Sign-off Form,* which requires teacher candidates to acknowledge "the ultimate responsibility for compiling the

documentation (including writing the commentaries) lies with the credential candidate" (http://pacttpa.org/_main/hub.php?pagename= Supporting_Documents_for_Candidates [PACT, 2008c]).

6. *California Standards Documents,* which provide links to the California Academic Content Standards for various subject areas found at the California Department of Education website (www.cde.ca.gov/be/st/ss/).

7. *Teaching Event Handbooks,* which provide candidates guidance in completing their Teaching Event in both multiple (elementary) and single subjects (secondary).

8. *Rubrics,* which explain to candidates, faculty, student teaching supervisors, cooperating teachers, and assessors how each task of the Teaching Event is scored (www.pacttpa.org/_main/hub.php?pageName=Rubrics# Rubrics [PACT, 2008b, p. 1]).

Unacceptable Candidate Support in Completing the Teaching Event

According to information provided by the PACT consortium, these types of support are deemed unacceptable in faculty or program support of teacher candidates constructing the Teaching Event:

1. Choosing curriculum or instructional materials for the candidate
2. Providing one's own analysis of the candidate's students and artifacts
3. Offering alternative responses to commentary prompts ("do this instead")
4. Suggesting specific changes for the Teaching Event rather than asking probative or clarifying questions that help candidates reach their own conclusions
5. Providing intensive coaching aimed at helping candidates perceived as weak to pass the Teaching Event
6. Editing the Teaching Event, or providing any kind of direct written drafts or revisions for the candidate. (Stansbury, 2006, p. 3)

The Unified Learning Segment in the PACT Teaching Event

According to the information on the **unified learning segment** in the *Overview of the PACT Teaching Event* provided in each TE Handbook, "A learning segment is a set of lessons that build upon one another toward a central focus that reflects key concepts and skills, with a clearly defined beginning and end" (http://pacttpa.org/_main/hub/php?pagename= Teaching_Event_Handbooks#Handbooks [PACT, 2008d]). The learning segment can be part of a larger instructional unit, and for candidates on block scheduling, additional instruction within the time period not included in the learning segment is permissible. The focus of the learning segment should be on only one class, even if the candidate teaches the subject to more than one class.

Candidates are then instructed to "plan a learning segment of about one week (approximately three to five hours of instruction) that is designed to support students in developing an understanding of the subject. . . . The learning segment must include learning objectives for both curriculum content and the development of academic language related to that content" (http://pacttpa.org/_main/hub/php?pagename=Teaching_Event_Handbooks#Handbooks [PACT, 2008d]).

● Submitting the Unified Learning Segment

The PACT Teaching Event Handbooks (http://pacttpa.org) ask candidates to submit teaching artifacts and analysis with these components:

1. Lesson plans, copies of instructional and assessment materials, two video clips of teaching, a summary of whole class learning, and an analysis of student work samples
2. Written commentaries describing teaching context, analyzing teaching practices, and reflecting on what was learned about teaching practices and students' learning

The instructions in the Teaching Event Handbooks guide candidates in compiling the instructional materials, video selection, student work samples, and commentaries required in the Teaching Event (http://pacttpa.org/_main/hub/php?pagename=Teaching_Event_Handbooks#Handbooks [PACT, 2008d]).

● How the Unified Learning Segment Prompts Vary by Subject and Grade Level

Prompts for learning segment artifacts and video clips vary by subject and area of specialization (multiple or single subject). In multiple subjects (elementary), candidates focus on either literacy or mathematics then choose two tasks for further planning, instruction, assessment, and reflection from literacy, mathematics, history/social science, and science. According to

PACT information on multiple subjects, the scores from the Teaching Event are combined with scores from the Subject Matter Tasks in core content areas to determine whether Multiple-Subjects candidates pass the PACT Teaching Event (www.pacttpa.org/_main/hub.php?pageName= Supporting_Documents_for_Candidates [PACT, 2008c]).

The prompts for the learning segment in each content area and area of specialization—multiple or single subject—are available in the Teaching Event Handbooks (http://pacttpa.org). Examine Table 2.3 for examples of subject-specific differences in the Teaching Events (Stansbury, 2008, pp. 1–3).

● Video Clip Requirements for the PACT Instruction Task

The topic, length, and number of video clips vary by subject area and grade level. Almost all subjects require two video clips of no more than 10 minutes each, showing the student teacher in the classroom setting. In contrast, multiple-subject math candidates prepare one 15-minute video clip of teaching performance. In general, the video clips require teacher candidates to demonstrate how they (1) engage students in learning specific skills and strategies to comprehend the basic precepts of the topic, laying the foundation for activities and assessments, and (2) interact with students as a whole group, in small group activities, and one-on-one, with pedagogically and developmentally appropriate responses to students' questions, comments, and needs (Stansbury, 2008).

Videotaping Support for Candidates

In its "Supporting Documents for Candidates" section, the PACT website provides two helpful documents on videotaping: *PACT Videotaping Policies* and *Procedures for Videotaping* (http://pacttpa.org/_main/hub.php? pageName=Supporting_Documents_for_Candidates [PACT, 2008c]).

The *PACT Videotaping Policies* document explains to candidates that the PACT consortium will use the materials in the Teaching Event as "data for a study of the technical quality of the Teaching Event as an assessment tool" (2008c, p. 1) and reminds teacher candidates that Teaching Event materials will be used to:

- Conduct research related to the validity and reliability of the Teaching Event as an assessment

TABLE **2.3**

Learning Segment Prompts by Different Subjects/Grade Levels

Subject Area	**Focus of Learning Segment** **(Candidate provides opportunities for students to . . .)**
Agriculture (General and Technology/Design)	Use facts, concepts, strategies, and skills to produce a product relevant to agricultural technology/design.
Agriculture (Economic Emphasis)	Use facts, concepts, and interpretations to make and explain judgments about a significant economic phenomenon relevant to agriculture.
Agriculture (Science Emphasis)	Use agriculture-related scientific concepts to make sense of one or more real-world phenomena by using key inquiry skills.
Art	(1) Make art (creative expression); (2) Analyze, interpret, and evaluate qualities of visual form (artistic perception); (3) Understand the contributions artists and art make to culture and society (historical and cultural context); and (4) Understand how people make and justify judgments about art objects (aesthetic valuing).
Bilingual Elementary Literacy	Comprehend and/or compose text by developing literacy skills and strategies.
Bilingual Elementary Mathematics	Use the language(s) of instruction to develop your students' conceptual understanding, computational/procedural fluency, and mathematical reasoning skills.
Elementary Literacy	Develop students' ability to comprehend and/or compose text by developing literacy skills and strategies.
Elementary Mathematics	Develop students' conceptual understanding, computational/procedural fluency, and mathematical reasoning skills.
English-Language Arts	Support students in developing an understanding and interpretation of complex text and in creating a written product responding to text.
History/Social Science	Use facts, concepts, and interpretations to make and explain judgments about a significant historical event or social science phenomenon.
Health Science	Develop students' abilities to analyze the effects of their behaviors on their own and/or others' health or well-being.
Mathematics	Develop students' mathematical knowledge by developing a balance of procedural fluency, conceptual understanding, and mathematical reasoning.
Music	Develop students' musical skills of artistic perception, creative expression, historical and cultural content, aesthetic valuing, and/or connections, relations, and applications.

(continues)

TABLE **2.3** (*continued*)

Subject Area	Focus of Learning Segment (Candidate provides opportunities for students to . . .)
Physical Education	Meet one of the Physical Education Model Content Standards for California Public Schools specifically to demonstrate knowledge and competency in motor skills, movement patterns, and strategies needed to perform one or more specific physical activities.
Science	Develop students' abilities to use scientific concepts to make sense of one or more real-world phenomena by using key scientific inquiry skills.
World Languages	Develop and demonstrate communicative proficiency (both productive and receptive) in the target language and familiarity with cultures that use that language.

Source: Stansbury (2008), pp 1–3.

- Train scorers, including college/university faculty and distinguished classroom teachers
- Inform potential professional development of supervisors and cooperating teachers to prepare them to better assist teacher candidates in completing Teaching Events
- Improve the fit between the Teaching Event, coursework within the teacher preparation program, and the context of the student or intern teaching

These policies and procedures also caution candidates about the confidential nature of their PACT materials and videotapes. Candidates are reminded that materials used for the purposes of completing the Teaching Event should not contain any identifying information on the names of students or the school site. Candidates, scorers, cooperating teachers, and university supervisors are not allowed to discuss the content of the videotapes or materials outside a professional development workshop or scoring session (http://pacttpa.org/_main/hub.php?pageName=Supporting_Documents_for_Candidates [PACT, 2008c, p. 1]).

Each teacher preparation program at PACT-aligned institutions also provides teacher candidates with videotaping policies, procedures, and tips. Classes, websites, and/or workshops are provided to aid candidates in creating the best-quality video and audio possible in a classroom setting.

Many of the institutions have a check-out procedure for digital video cameras and microphones as well.

The *Procedures for Videotaping* guide reminds candidates not to expect "a Hollywood production," and provides practical and logistical tips on how to videotape their lessons for the Teaching Event (http://pacttpa.org/_main/hub.php?pageName=Supporting_Documents_for_Candidates [PACT, 2008c, p. 1]).

Confidentiality of Videotaped Classroom Students

Almost all California school districts and schools have a videotape permission form or parental notification letter. The state superintendent, Jack O'Connell, also sent a letter to all district superintendents, explaining the key features of PACT and requesting each district's cooperation in the classroom videotaping efforts at the various public school sites (http://www.cde.ca.gov/).

If a district or school does not have its own videotape permission form, candidates may obtain one from their teacher preparation program, such as the sample parental notification letter in Figure 2.2.

FIGURE **2.2**

Sample Parental Notification Letter

Dear Parent/Guardian:

This semester, your child's class is working with a student teacher, _____, from California State University Orange Tree. All student teachers must complete the PACT, or Performance Assessment for California Teachers. The PACT requires a 15- to 20- minute video clip of one or more lessons to focus on the student teacher's instruction, not on the students in the class. The video clip(s) will be assessed by university faculty to assess the student teacher's performance and to evaluate our program. Student teachers also collect samples of student work, but no pupil names appear on any of these materials, and **all materials are kept confidential.**

Please sign and return this Permission Form to indicate your permission for these actions.

Thank you for your consideration.

Cordially,
Teacher Preparation Program Coordinator

Differences in Video Clips among Subjects and Grade Levels

Task 3, Overview of Task for the PACT Teaching Event, notes the differences among subject and grade-level areas, with regard to the required length and number of video clips:

> Note that there are one or two video clips, with the elementary areas and mathematics giving candidates a choice between one or two clips, art requiring three video clips, and agricultural technology/design allowing up to five (since instructors often rotate between four stations centered around different types of machinery, spending a brief period of time at each). The total time varies: 15 minutes total to 10 minutes per clip or 20 minutes total. (Stansbury, 2008, p. 3)

● Uploading a Lesson Plan to an Electronic/Digital Platform

Figure 2.3 provides a sample lesson plan template format (Lesson Builder) used by California State University, Northridge, single-subject candidates in TaskStream's (www.taskstream.com) electronic portfolio management system. Digital portfolio systems vary by campus across the state. Candidates upload their lesson plan because it is a critical part of the unified learning segment in the PACT Teaching Event.

By clicking on the interactive buttons labeled designer, summary, grade/level, and so forth, candidates receive a brief prompt that guides their entry choices for that area of the lesson plan builder template. These prompts are meant to explain what is being asked of the candidate in the lesson plan and encourage further thought and inquiry toward completion of the learning segment in the PACT Teaching Event.

● The PACT Teaching Event and Electronic Portfolio Management Systems

All the required pieces of a PACT Teaching Event may be uploaded to TaskStream (www.taskstream), where the Teaching Event will be evaluated by trained PACT scorers at the candidate's institution. It should be noted that not all PACT-aligned institutions use TaskStream.

Each required section of the PACT Teaching Event electronic portfolio management system offers candidates specific directions and detailed lists

FIGURE **2.3**

Sample Lesson Plan Builder Format in TaskStream

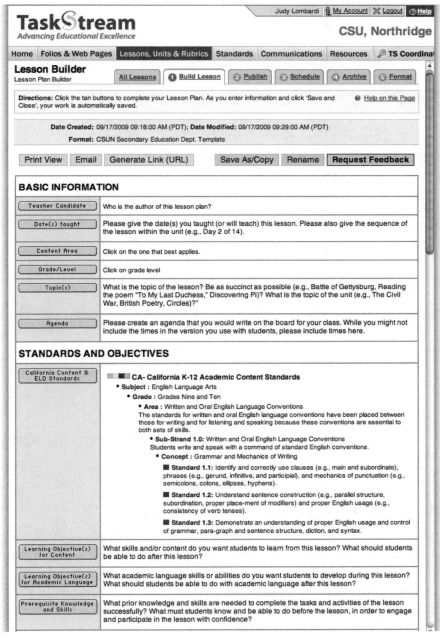

(continues)

FIGURE **2.3** (*continued*)

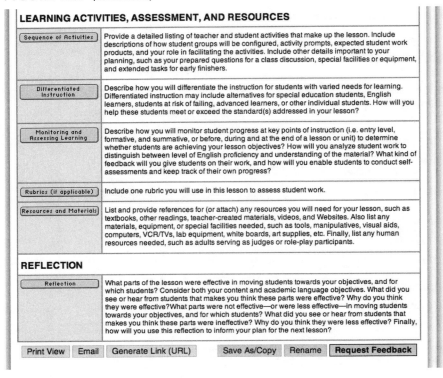

LEARNING ACTIVITIES, ASSESSMENT, AND RESOURCES	
Sequence of Activities	Provide a detailed listing of teacher and student activities that make up the lesson. Include descriptions of how student groups will be configured, activity prompts, expected student work products, and your role in facilitating the activities. Include other details important to your planning, such as your prepared questions for a class discussion, special facilities or equipment, and extended tasks for early finishers.
Differentiated Instruction	Describe how you will differentiate the instruction for students with varied needs for learning. Differentiated instruction may include alternatives for special education students, English learners, students at risk of failing, advanced learners, or other individual students. How will you help these students meet or exceed the standard(s) addressed in your lesson?
Monitoring and Assessing Learning	Describe how you will monitor student progress at key points of instruction (i.e. entry level, formative, and summative, or before, during and at the end of a lesson or unit) to determine whether students are achieving your lesson objectives? How will you analyze student work to distinguish between level of English proficiency and understanding of the material? What kind of feedback will you give students on their work, and how will you enable students to conduct self-assessments and keep track of their own progress?
Rubrics (if applicable)	Include one rubric you will use in this lesson to assess student work.
Resources and Materials	List and provide references for (or attach) any resources you will need for your lesson, such as textbooks, other readings, teacher-created materials, videos, and Websites. Also list any materials, equipment, or special facilities needed, such as tools, manipulatives, visual aids, computers, VCR/TVs, lab equipment, white boards, art supplies, etc. Finally, list any human resources needed, such as adults serving as judges or role-play participants.

REFLECTION	
Reflection	What parts of the lesson were effective in moving students towards your objectives, and for which students? Consider both your content and academic language objectives. What did you see or hear from students that makes you think these parts were effective? Why do you think they were effective?What parts were not effective—or were less effective—in moving students towards your objectives, and for which students? What did you see or hear from students that makes you think these parts were ineffective? Why do you think they were less effective? Finally, how will you use this reflection to inform your plan for the next lesson?

| Print View | Email | Generate Link (URL) | | Save As/Copy | Rename | **Request Feedback** |

Source: Reprinted with permission from TaskStream, LLC. Copyright 2006.

of required items, to ensure candidates understand the process and submit the necessary PACT documents and video clip(s).

● Evaluation and Scoring of the PACT Teaching Event

More information on scoring, rubrics, and assessment data can be found in Chapter 4. The Teaching Event Context piece is read by evaluators but not scored, as it is considered a foundational writing task for the four pillar tasks to come (Planning, Instruction, Assessment, and Reflection). In addition, the authenticity form, which verifies that candidates are submitting their own work, is noted as simply present or absent.

Candidates Who Do Not Pass the Teaching Event

PACT-aligned teacher preparation programs have policies and procedures to assist struggling candidates in revising and resubmitting tasks. Faculty members, university supervisors, student teaching coordinators, and other knowledgeable participants at an institution may meet with the candidate, ask probing and clarifying questions to bring about a better result, and review areas of concern. They may not make direct revisions for the candidate (http://pacttpa.org [PACT, 2008a]).

The emphasis is on helping the candidate to improve past outcomes for maximal success and learn to be the best teacher possible. More information on remediation features can be found in Chapter 4.

Summary

What does the Teaching Event tell PACT-aligned institutions about their candidates' teaching performance? Aligned with the California Teaching Performance Expectations (TPEs), state standards, and curricular frameworks, the PACT Teaching Event shows that candidates can "demonstrate their readiness for a full-time teaching assignment" (Stansbury, 2006, p. 1).

Teacher preparation programs can also use the PACT Teaching Event outcomes and technical data to assess the strengths and weaknesses of their own programs and identify areas in which teacher candidates need additional instruction and guidance.

The Teaching Event includes a sweeping scope of Context, Planning, Instruction, Assessment, and Reflection, with Academic Language addressed across all tasks. Depth of reflection and analysis, connections among tasks, evidentiary artifacts, student work samples, and video clips all demonstrate the candidate's classroom teaching performance in an authentic classroom setting.

References

California Department of Education (CDE). (2007). *Standards documents.* Retrieved December 1, 2007, from www.cde.ca.gov/be/st/ss/.

California Commission on Teacher Credentialing (CCTC). (2001, 2008). Retrieved January 15, 2009, from www.ctc.ca.gov/.

California Commission on Teacher Credentialing (CCTC). (2001). *Teachers meeting standards for professional certification in California: Second annual report.* Retrieved December 1, 2007, from www.ctc.ca.gov/reports/ab471/report.pdf.

G*Star Electronic Portfolio System. (2006). University of California, Riverside. Retrieved October 27, 2007, from https://www.gstar.ucr.edu/gstar2006/AboutGSTAR.ppt.

Live Text. (2009). Retrieved February 26, 2009, from https://college.livetext.com/.

Making Good Choices. (2008). Retrieved March 4, 2009, from www.pacttpa.org/_files/Supporting_Documents/Making%20Good%20Choices%204.11.08.doc.

Nagle, J. (2008). *Performance assessment for California teachers (PACT) teaching event: Using a state accountability measure of teaching to enhance critically reflective practice.* Retrieved January 3, 2009, from www.allacademic.com/meta/p_mla_apa_research_citation/0/3/5/8/7/p35871_index.html.

PACT. (2008a). *PACT consortium website.* Retrieved January 6, 2009, from http://pacttpa .org.

PACT. (2008b). *PACT rubrics.* Retrieved January 30, 2009, from www.pacttpa.org/_main/hub .php?pageName=Rubrics#Rubrics.

PACT. (2008c). *Supporting documents for candidates: Teaching event handbooks and rubrics.* Retrieved January 5, 2009, from http://pacttpa.org/_main/hub.php?pageName= Supporting_Documents_for_Candidates.

PACT. (2008d). *Teaching event handbooks.* Retrieved January 15, 2009, from http:// pacttpa.org/_main/hub.php?pageName=Teaching_Event_Handbooks#Handbooks.

PACT Teaching Event. (2008). University of San Diego. Retrieved January 5, 2009, from www.sandiego.edu/soles/programs/learning_and_teaching/credential_programs/ pact_teaching_event.php.

Pecheone, R. (2008). *The thinking behind PACT: Performance assessment for California teachers.* Retrieved January 6, 2008, from http://pacttpa.org/_files/Publications_and_ Presentations/PACT.ppt.

Pecheone, R., and Chung, R. (2006). Evidence in teacher education: The performance Assessment for California Teachers (PACT). *Journal of Teacher Education 57,* 22–36. Retrieved June 11, 2007, from http://pacttpa.org/_files/Publications_and_Presentations/ PACT_Evidence_Teacher_Ed_JTE.pdf.

Stanford University School of Education. (2007). *PACT teaching event overview.* Retrieved December 1, 2007, from www.susestep.stanford.edu/elementary/handbook_documents/PACT%20Teaching%20Event%20Overview.doc.

Stansbury, K. (2008). PACT 101: Deconstructing the teaching event. Presentation at PACT Consortium Conference, University of California at Santa Barbara, November 13.

Stansbury, K. (2006). English language arts teaching event candidate handbook 2008–09. Paper presented at PACT Consortium Conference, University of California at Santa Barbara, November 13, 2008.

TaskStream. (2008). *Accountability management system.* Retrieved January 4, 2009, from www.taskstream.com/pub/.

TaskStream. (2008). *Lesson plan builder.* Retrieved January 2, 2008, from www.taskstream. com/Main/main_frame.asp.

Teachscape. (2008). Retrieved January 18, 2009, from http://teachscape.com/html/ts/nps/ index.html.

Understanding Academic Language

The term *Academic Language* encompasses all the language demands placed on school-age learners. These language demands range from subject-specialized vocabulary to the oral and written formats used in varying subjects to the linguistic features and text types of different disciplines. Each discipline requires learners to understand and apply different vocabulary to access them successfully, as seen in Figure 3.1.

Types of words, terms, and vocabulary occur in each specific content area as well, as seen in Table 3.1.

Academic Language goes well beyond specialized vocabulary, however, and embraces a wide array of language demands placed on learners. A formal definition of *Academic Language* is "the language that is used by teachers and students for the purpose of acquiring new knowledge and skills . . . imparting new information, describing abstract ideas, and developing students' conceptual understanding" (Chamot & O'Malley, 1994, p. 40).

Academic Language includes both the receptive (listening, reading) and productive-expressive (speaking, writing) language students must employ in understanding the material and conveying their thoughts in oral, written, or multimedia form. Academic Language also addresses the operational, organizational structures of language, as well as the functions of language (Bailey, 2007).

When students engage with school textbooks and other materials, they "engage in the communication related to the activity: listen to directions,

FIGURE **3.1**

Academic Language: Examples of Specialized Vocabulary

- Art: composition, medium, perspective
- Business: amortization, broker, proposal
- English: genre, essay, journal
- Foreign languages: audio-lingual, dialogue, fluency
- Kinesiology: aerobics, body type, heart rate
- Math: additive, binomial, denominator
- Music: orchestration, notes, coda
- Science: species, condensation, hypothesis
- Social sciences: era, civilization, timeline

read a piece of text, answer a question out loud, prepare a presentation, write a summary, respond to written questions, research a topic, talk within a small group of peers. All of these common activities create a demand for language reception or language production" (Sato & Curtis, 2005, p. 25). Lab reports, essays, reading comprehension tasks, mathematical problem solving, physical education activities, music lessons, art projects, technology products—all require specific vocabulary, terminology, and communication skills in order for learners to access and apply them with confidence.

TABLE **3.1**

Vocabulary Used in Social Studies

Types of Words	Examples
Content words pertaining to social studies (concept words)	city-state, legend, democracy, golden age, empire, republic, balance of power
Everyday vocabulary with special meanings in social studies	ancient, concept, culture, decline, rivalry, ruler, territory, estates
Difficult expressions for English language learners and struggling readers	led to, in order to, touched off, dug in for; prepositions; and words that express logical relationships

Source: Reading Institute for Academic Preparedness (2007). Reprinted with permission.

The Role of Academic Language in the PACT Teaching Event

The single pillar of learning that is embedded in and forms an overarching task for all the others in the PACT Teaching Event is Academic Language. Teacher candidates are expected to address language demands, as they apply Academic Language to all the other required tasks of the Teaching Event. Teacher candidates are also expected to demonstrate they know the difference between strategies for content learning and those that specifically target language development.

The PACT scoring form, or rubric, addresses Academic Language by asking guiding questions in two areas: (1) Item 11, Understanding Language Demands: How does the candidate describe the language demands of the learning tasks and assessments in relation to student language development? and (2) Item 12, Supporting Academic Language Development: How do the candidate's planning, instruction, and assessment support academic language development? (http://pacttpa.org [PACT, 2008]).

The PACT Teaching Event recognizes the crucial role of the teacher in helping pupils understand and apply the language demands of the various disciplines, texts, materials, and assignments. Educational experts recognize that language demands go beyond the basics of reading, writing, speaking, and listening skills, because "so much of what we do outside of narratives is tied to vocabulary—a water table is different from a math table is different from tabling a motion" (Alvermann, in McGrath, 2005, p. 1).

In its *Making Good Choices* document for candidates and trained scorers, the PACT consortium defines Academic Language, describes the language demands of school, and explains what developing Academic Language means with regard to the Teaching Event (Sato & Curtis, 2005). Academic Language is emphasized in Task 2 of the Teaching Event, Planning, where candidates must describe the strategies they used to identify, address, and later assess Academic Language in assignments and other learner tasks.

Challenges in Teaching Academic Language

The PACT consortium acknowledges that defining and applying Academic Language can be challenging for candidates in the Teaching Event and even for trained scorers to identify and evaluate successfully (Stansbury, 2008). Teacher roles in Academic Language include these key elements:

1. Analyze what makes the language demanding for individuals or groups.
2. Develop scaffolds and supports to help students understand and apply academic language.
3. Use strategies to develop proficiency in academic language and provide rationale for strategies. (Scarcella, 2003)

As students go through their school day, moving from one subject to another, the language demands, the type of information received and produced, even the modes of interacting with texts, teachers, materials, and other learners, change. As a result of this variety across subjects and tasks, Academic Language is not just a term for teachers of struggling readers and English learners, but one that addresses the language demands for all learners in all disciplines (Bailey, 2007).

Even when teaching candidates note in the PACT Teaching Event that there are no officially designated or redesignated English learners in their classrooms, the premise of Academic Language still proposes that candidates pay attention to language development needs among all learners. Both comprehension and production are central to the language development process. Candidates must realize that the strategies they provide to support content learning need to be augmented or modified to support language development. Teacher candidates who view the curriculum samples and pedagogy surrounding Academic Language come to realize that the associated strategies may enhance learning for all students.

Another challenge in understanding Academic Language is that although second language development and linguistics have a long, rich history of research and available information, Academic Language has just recently been emphasized and described. As such, the features of Academic Language are still being examined by educational experts in relation to teaching practices and learning outcomes (Bailey, 2007).

Examples of Academic Language versus Simplified Language

Teachers want students to understand text and oral presentations, but simplifying language for students does not help them acquire the language of school. The problem with oversimplifying text for students is that "instruction that is easy for English learners to understand may help students understand the gist of concepts *but not give them a deep understanding of the concepts*" (Scarcella, 2003, p. 10). All learners should be given specific, structured, direct opportunities to recognize, understand, and apply Academic Language within the given context. Table 3.2 offers an example of academic language compared to simplified language.

Understanding the need for both academic and simplified language is crucial to the candidate's operationalizing both types effectively in the classroom setting, as evidenced in the PACT Teaching Event. Academic Language experts view it as critical to effective teaching, because Academic Language "is a key factor in the achievement gap between high- and low-performing students. Content area teachers across the curriculum can play an essential role in reducing this gap with an increased awareness of the need to boost Academic Language skills of low performing students from a diverse range of language and cultural backgrounds" (Zwiers, 2008, p. 1).

How Experts Define and Describe Academic Language

Based on the work of Cummins (1979, 1981, 2000), Canale and Swain (1980), Chamot and O'Malley (1994), Kern (2000), Scarcella (2003), and Bailey (2007), the understanding, importance, and application of Academic Language has been building and continues to grow. Academic Language can now be seen as a second language for many students (Bailey, 2007). The presence of and emphasis on Academic Language in the PACT Teaching Event and scoring form attest to its rising importance as a key component of quality teaching.

TABLE **3.2**

Academic versus Simplified Language

Academic Language	Simplified Language
Jupiter is the largest planet in the solar system. Its diameter is 88,846 miles (142,984 kilometers), more than 11 times that of Earth and about one-tenth that of the sun. It would take more than 1,000 Earths to fill up the volume of the giant planet. When viewed from Earth, Jupiter appears brighter than most stars. It is usually the second brightest planet—after Venus.	Jupiter is a big, big planet. Jupiter is very bright.

Source: Scarcella (2003, pp. 69–70). Reprinted with permission.

In 1981, Cummins introduced evidence of BICS and CALP occurring in schools (basic interpersonal communicative skills and cognitive academic language proficiency) (Cummins, 2008). A distinction was made between the social, conversational aspects of language, or BICS, and the academic proficiency required for school, CALP. According to Cummins:

> The distinction was intended to draw attention to the very different time periods typically required by immigrant children to acquire conversational fluency in their second language as compared to grade-appropriate academic proficiency in that language. Conversational fluency is often acquired to a functional level within about two years of initial exposure to the second language whereas at least five years is usually required to catch up to native speakers in academic aspects of the second language. . . . Failure to take account of the BICS/CALP (conversational/academic) distinction has resulted in *discriminatory psychological assessment of bilingual students* [emphasis added] and premature exit from language support programs . . . into mainstream classes. (2003, p. 1)

This initial distinction between social and Academic Language was the key to understanding why some students who demonstrated language fluency in social settings and conversations had difficulty in performing academic tasks. It should be noted that neither BICS nor CALP is considered superior to the other for communicative purposes; both are recognized as different ways of receiving and producing information and ideas (Cummins, 2000).

Chamot and O'Malley (1994) describe the language functions learners must be able to perform in the content areas with regard to communicative intent, such as explaining, describing, and contrasting. Their emphasis on the functions of language over the operations and organizational structures of language helps define the tasks students have to perform in a classroom setting and explicates the *what* versus the *how* of language reception and production.

Kern (2000) highlights three essential components of Academic Language: linguistic, cognitive, and sociocultural/psychological. His work argues that it is not possible to understand academic literacy without viewing it from these three perspectives, and that language practices are always deeply embedded in any social or cultural practice. The linguistic component includes phonological, lexical, grammatical, sociolinguistic, and discourse elements, based on the model of communicative competence (Canale & Swain, 1980) and explicated by Scarcella (2003, p. 21), as seen in Table 3.3.

Academic Language can also be described in terms of the elements of its cognitive component (Scarcella, 2003):

1. *Knowledge:*   Students who have acquired Academic Language can build on their previous years of reading and ideas, definitions, and stories.
2. *Higher-order thinking:*   Students can interpret, analyze, synthesize, apply, and evaluate text and other materials, written, oral, or multimedia.
3. *Strategic component:*   Students have strategies to enhance their communication skills and for accessing text such as paraphrasing, underlining, and using marginalia and highlighted notes.
4. *Metalinguistic awareness component:*   Students have the language resources to think about their thinking as expressed in written, oral, or multimedia form, including diction, editing, and use of reference and handbooks, spell checker and grammar functions in word processing and electronic communication.

The relationship between components occurs when students have a solid knowledge of everyday terms, vocabulary, structural, grammatical, and linguistic components and can then build on that knowledge to achieve mastery of Academic Language and increased skill in all forms of communication. Scarcella points out that "academic situations push learners to use language accurately" (2003, p. 29). Again, it should be noted that Academic Language is not better than everyday language or other forms of expression but has different contexts, purposes, and outcomes (Cummins, 2000).

To achieve mastery in Academic Language, learners must develop more than linguistic and cognitive components—they must develop the sociocultural and psychological dimensions of academic language. Vygotsky (1962, 1978) describes the importance of social interaction in children as critical to cognitive development and states that a key element in these early interactions is communication, which helps mediate social interactions.

Inherent in language are the norms, values, beliefs, and attitudes of the speaker and the related culture and community. Simply put, what is polite

TABLE **3.3**

Linguistic Components of Ordinary English versus Academic Language

Component	Ordinary English	Academic Language
Phonological	Knowledge of everyday words, sound combinations, stress, intonation, graphemes, spelling *Example:* chip vs. cheap	Knowledge of phonological features of academic English such as stress, intonation, sound patterns *Example:* geography, geographical
Lexical	Knowledge of the forms and meanings of words found in everyday situations, including prefixes, suffixes, root words, parts of speech, and grammatical strictures on words *Example:* find	Knowledge of the forms and meanings of words found in academic disciplines, including prefixes, suffixes, root words, parts of speech, and grammatical strictures on words *Example:* locate
Grammatical	Knowledge of morphemes, simple rules of punctuation, grammatical strictures on everyday words, grammatical features associated with words *Example:* child vs. children	Knowledge of grammar (morphemes and syntax) associated with argument, procedural description, definition, analysis, grammatical strictures on words, knowledge of more complex punctuation rules *Example:* criterion vs. criteria
Sociolinguistic	Knowledge of how sentences are produced, word functions and types of words in everyday situations, including greetings, common statements, and simple commands *Example:* How are you?	Knowledge of increased number of language functions, including elevated forms of apologizing, complaining, requesting, and knowledge of genres such as scientific writing *Example:* How do you do?
Discourse	Knowledge of the basic discourse devices used to introduce topics, keep conversation flowing, letters, lists, simple transitional signals in talk and writing *Examples:* And then, my next point is . . .	Knowledge of discourse features used in specific academic genres, transitions and organizational signals, and aids to gaining perspectives, seeing relationships, following logic *Examples:* Consequently, as a result of my findings, pursuant to

Source: Adapted from Scarcella (2005).

and acceptable in one language may be seen as rude or aggressive in another language. Certain gestures have loaded meanings in some languages, and storytelling may be linear in one language yet recursive or global in another. Exposure to learning other languages and types of discourse, both in home settings and at school, aids learners in understanding the perspectives of other languages and cultures. Students should be able to learn and apply Academic Language without rejecting their own home language, identity, or belief system (Gee, 1996).

Why Students Struggle with Academic Language

Although there is no "one-size-fits-all" for Academic Language challenges, here are some reasons Academic Language experts say some students face difficulties in that area:

1. Absence of exposure to books and to people who use Academic Language
2. Absence of opportunities to use Academic Language
3. Absence of motivation to develop and use Academic Language
4. Absence of solid instruction, including sufficient and supportive feedback
5. Absence of understanding what Academic Language is and when or how to apply it (Scarcella, 2003)

In addition, educational experts who inform Academic Language teaching practices are faced with an absence of conclusive research evidence on how social language impacts Academic Language learning, as well as a lack of longitudinal studies on the trajectory of Academic Language demands across grade levels (Scarcella, 2003; Bailey, 2007).

Academic Language Strategies for Candidates in the PACT Teaching Event

Academic Language empowers students in the language skills they need for school. If students have academic literacy, they can analyze information or arguments; synthesize information from several sources; provide short answer responses or essays; write to discover and learn new ideas; provide factual descriptions; narrate events or report facts; and infuse Academic Language into electronic communications and technology products (Scarcella, 2003).

Teaching does not have to be "either-or" (sacrificing clarity for the sake of using Academic Language, or the reverse). Effective teachers teach Academic Language and provide clear explanations of meaning; provide ample opportunities for students to practice using academic language; understand that content and language can and should be taught together; and recognize that conquering new language builds confidence in learners. According to Wong Fillmore and Snow (2000, p. 8), "Teachers need to understand how to design the classroom language environment so as to optimize language and literacy learning and *to avoid linguistic obstacles* [emphasis added] to content area learning."

In the PACT Teaching Event, candidates can integrate a number of strategies and practices into their teaching to help learners build Academic Language skills, as seen in Figure 3.2.

FIGURE **3.2**

Candidate Strategies to Address Academic Language in the Teaching Event

1. **Use frontloading.** Preteach challenging and difficult vocabulary, and engage learners in activities to understand the terms.
2. **Create visual representations.** Present or have students present ideas as a visual model, graphic organizer, or multimedia product.
3. **Bring Academic Language to the surface.** Teach students the term *Academic Language,* explain why it is important, and provide systematic instruction and examples.
4. **Share resources.** Teach students how to use heritage language/learner's dictionaries, memorization techniques, procedures for obtaining help, and test-taking strategies.
5. **Teach about textual evidence.** Show students how to use textual evidence to support their good ideas, and use multiple models of its application.
6. **Use explicit, scaffolded instruction.** Give clear instructions, both auditory and visually, and provide models of expected or possible outcomes.
7. **Examine learning outcomes.** Interactive strategies are great, but candidates should ask themselves, Is there any real learning going on, or is this just a fun activity?
8. **Assess students' Academic Language through multiple measures.** Use both pre-made (worksheets) and authentic (essays, portfolios) assessments.
9. **Use strategies wisely.** Teachers do not have to show the whole movie, when just a clip will do, and should explore the range of strategies available through differentiated instruction.
10. **Explore resources.** Candidates can acquaint themselves with the rich array of online and text materials currently available on Academic Language and share them with students.
11. **Provide meaningful feedback.** Give students supportive feedback, including student–teacher conferences, on their use of Academic Language, suggesting specific ways they can improve their understanding and application of it.

Note: Created with assistance from Scarcella (2003).

Questions about Academic Language That Candidates Must Address

Candidates must answer questions about Academic Language in various sections of the Teaching Event, for example in single subjects English language arts, as seen in Table 3.4. The guiding statements and questions are tied to the TPEs, or Teaching Performance Expectations, described in Chapter 1.

Examples of Candidate Responses to Academic Language in the Teaching Event

The four vignettes provided here from Teaching Events in English language arts demonstrate how candidates might answer a question on Academic Language, with responses scored from Level 1 (low on scoring form) to Level 4 (high on scoring form). These examples are based on the Academic Language guiding question from the Planning task on language development, "Consider aspects of English language proficiency development in conversational and Academic Language as well as in the students' primary language, if other than English. Describe the language development of your entire class, not just your English learners":

Candidate Response at Level 1

The language level of the task requires more than skimming. I have two worksheets for vocabulary study. The lesson will focus on having students use their imagination to figure out the context clues for words they don't understand. I think I have some English learners, but I have not had a chance to ask my master teacher or look at any records yet. I'll just make sure they can see and hear all the words I use. I also need to meet with my teacher to get some ideas from research to support my work.

Candidate Response at Level 2

In my classroom, the class records show that there are currently no designated or redesignated English learners, so English language proficiency appears to be high. The students' level of social interaction and conversation, based on Vygotsky's social interaction theory (1962), indicates that most

TABLE **3.4**

Questions on Academic Language in the Teaching Event

Task	Focus Area	Guiding Statement/Question
Context	Language development	Consider aspects of English language proficiency development in conversational and academic language as well as in the students' primary language, if other than English. Describe the language development of your entire class, not just your English learners. (TPEs 7, 8)
Planning	Theoretical framework/ research	Briefly describe the theoretical framework/research that informs your instructional design for developing your students' knowledge and abilities in both English language arts and academic language during the learning segment. (TPEs 10, 11, 12, 13)
Planning	Learning tasks	How do key learning tasks in your plan build on each other to support student learning of how to understand, interpret, and respond to complex text, and to develop related academic language? Describe specific strategies that you will use to build student learning across the learning segment. Reference the instructional materials you have included, as needed. (TPEs 1, 4, 9)
Planning	Language demands	What language demands of the learning and assessment tasks are likely to be challenging for your students at different levels of language development? (Language demands can be related to vocabulary, features of text types such as narrative or expository text, or other language demands such as understanding oral presentations.) Explain how specific features of the learning and assessment tasks in your plan support students in meeting these language demands, building on what your students are currently able to do with language. Be sure to set these support plans in the context of your long-term goals for your students' development of academic language. (TPE 7)
Planning	Special needs	Describe any teaching strategies you have planned for your students who have identified educational needs, such as English learners, Gifted and Talented Education (GATE), students with Individual Education Plans (IEPs). If you do not have any English learners, select a student who is challenged by academic English. Examples may include students who speak varieties of English or special-needs learners with receptive or expressive language difficulties. (TPEs 9, 12)

Task	Focus Area	Guiding Statement/Question
Instruction	Language supports	Describe any language supports used in the [video] clip to help your students, including English learners as well as other students struggling with language, understand the content and/or academic language central to the lesson. If possible, give one or two examples from the video clip of how you implemented these supports. (TPEs 4, 7)
Assessment	Language proficiency	From the three students whose work samples were selected, choose two students, at least one of which is an English learner. For these two students, describe their prior knowledge of the content and their individual learning challenges, e.g., academic development, language proficiency, special needs. What did you conclude about their learning during the learning segment? Cite evidence from the work samples and other classroom assessments relevant to the same evaluative criteria (or rubric). (TPE 3)
Reflection	Learning differences	When you consider the content learning of your students and the development of their academic language, what do you think explains the learning or differences in learning that you observed during the learning segment? Cite relevant research or theory that explains what you observed. (TPEs 7, 8, 13)
Reflection	Learning differences	Based on your experience teaching this learning segment, what did you learn about your students as learners, e.g., easy/difficult concepts and skills, easy/difficult learning tasks, easy/difficult features of academic language, common misunderstandings. Please cite specific evidence from previous Teaching Event tasks, as well as specific research and theories that inform your analysis. (TPE 3)

Source: http://pacttpa.org.

want to engage in active conversations about the lesson or other topics. During preteaching, I introduce difficult or challenging words, through graphic organizers, word games, and a class word wall, to help them access the text and assignments. I have explained Academic Language to my students. When I explain new terms and difficult vocabulary, I remind students that these words are part of Academic Language. Three to four students have started asking me on their own if the words we are using for a particular assignment are Academic Language, and I'm hoping that over time, more students will ask the same question.

Candidate Response at Level 3

The challenge with my students, both English proficient and English learners, is that they have a difficult time distinguishing between academic and informal language. I am using the work of Cummins (1981, 2000) to teach them the differences between academic and everyday language, and I told them one is not better than the other, just different. Using the work of Scarcella (2003), I have already explained what Academic Language is to my students, provided them with examples/models, and asked them to provide their own examples. According to class records, 80 percent of my class are English speakers, and the other 20 percent are designated or re-designated English learners. Almost all the class uses colloquial language, slang, and text messaging shortcuts in their writing and exams. I use real examples from student writing and speech to show them the differences between their language and Academic Language. I have also modeled the uses of rhetoric and how to write/speak for specific audiences and purposes, based on the *Rhetoric of Aristotle*. We have written about (in journals, essays, and graphic organizers) and discussed (in whole class, small group, and pair-shares) the differences between formal and informal language, and when/how the types of language should be applied. Students in my class with high levels of English proficiency do not seem to struggle with Academic Language and use new vocabulary right away in their assignments.

Candidate Response at Level 4

My research on teaching strategies is based on the fact that 90 percent of the students in this class perform at Basic or Below Basic in comprehension and writing, as evidenced by class records and formal state assessments. Almost all of the students have effective conversational English skills when they speak in social interactions and discussions during class. Spanish conventions for writing are apparent in 90 percent of students' writing as well, but direct, frequent grammar instruction assists students in performing well on in-class writing tasks and state grammar assessments. Using ideas from Scarcella (2003) on direct instruction, I conference with my students and conduct mini-lessons on patterns of error, reinforcing areas in which they do well. The same 90 percent of students struggle with academic vocabulary, even though they have received previous instruction in terms and vocabulary, which indicates a need for increased practice and multiple models/activities in Academic Language. I have used Joy Reid's *Teaching ESL Writing* (1993) and teaching strategies from the CARLA website, the Center for Research on Language Acquisition. These students need consistent and continuous scaffolding in vocabulary and grammar conventions for written English, and for this area, I have used the work of Alvermann, Elbow, Murray, Graves, and Burke. The school's high percentage of low-income and ELL students (92 percent) indicates an emphasis is needed on sheltered (SDAIE, Specifically Designed Academic Instruction in English) strategies and vocabulary development strategies. My lesson design includes SDAIE strategies such as confirmation and clarification checks, repetition and expansion, word banks, graphic organizers, and hands-on activities. For the 10 percent of students in my class who have advanced English proficiency, Academic Language is not an issue (i.e., they use the standard English conventions in their writing and grasp/apply the concepts of academic language easily). They readily apply new vocabulary to assignments and in-class discussions and enjoy learning about the nuances of mechanics, such as when to use a semicolon.

Brief Analysis of Vignettes

The Level 1 candidate response provides minimal support for student language development needs, indicates the candidate is not fully aware of the language development needs of learners, and lacks a range of explicit strategies to support Academic Language.

At Level 2, the candidate identifies some strategies for addressing language needs of learners but has not explained the role of Academic Language fully to students. Because designated English learners are not present, the candidate assumes and ignores the need for deeper and more effective language development strategies.

The Level 3 candidate uses statistics to describe the learner population and research to support the selected range of Academic Language strategies. The candidate discusses students who are highly proficient in Academic Language but needs to specifically target the needs of struggling readers and present more strategies for English learners. Strategies facilitate content learning but may not fully support language development.

At Level 4, the candidate uses statistics to describe Academic Language needs and research to support selected strategies for English learners. The candidate uses a range of strategies along a continuum of students' strengths and weaknesses in Academic Language. The Level 4 candidate demonstrates confidence about what is needed to boost language proficiency, how it can be supported, and why Academic Language is important to learning.

In these examples of PACT Teaching Event responses, candidates are scored on the quality and depth of thought and analysis, rather than the length of their response. Candidates with longer responses, however, tend to include more facts, details, and examples to support their ideas. Please see Chapter 4 for a discussion of how the PACT Teaching Event is scored, including an explanation of the criteria for the four-level scoring system.

Assisting Candidates with Academic Language

In its *Making Good Choices* document, PACT provides a definition of Academic Language and explains how it can be incorporated into the Teaching Event (www.srnleads.org/data/pdfs/pact.pdf). Member institutions provide information on Academic Language in their teacher preparation programs through coursework, and some programs offer special training seminars or workshops for candidates.

Candidates are also given opportunities to apply Academic Language across various disciplines and grade levels in completing their course assignments. Practice for candidates in understanding and teaching Academic Language is a key feature of many literacy and methods courses in PACT-aligned institutions.

Summary

Academic Language is the language used in the academic subjects of school. Academic Language helps learners to access, understand, and apply information, ideas, and concepts in a meaningful way. In school, language demands are placed on learners that differ from the conventions of social, conversational language. Helping learners distinguish and apply the difference between social and Academic Language can help boost their performance on assignments and informal and formal assessments, including standardized tests.

Teachers often design tasks and activities with certain Academic Language demands already embedded, so that direct, explicit teaching for Academic Language helps raise to the surface the language demands placed on learners. In the PACT Teaching Event, successful candidates must first identify the language demands and needs of their learners, and then plan, instruct, assess, and reflect on the strategies they use to address Academic Language. Their pedagogical choices must also be firmly based on research from Academic Language experts and content area specialists.

In acknowledging the importance of Academic Language in the Teaching Event and applying it to all tasks and areas, the PACT consortium recognizes the complexity of language, the different functions and roles of language, and the language demands on learners. Candidates who can effectively identify and address Academic Language in the Teaching Event, regardless of grade level or content area, can help their students be more successful in accessing, understanding, and applying the language of school.

References

Alvermann, D. E. (2001). In D. McGrath (Ed.). (2005). *Effective literacy instruction for adolescents.* Chicago: National Reading Conference.

Bailey, A. L. (2007). *The language demands of school: Putting academic language to the test.* New Haven, CT: Yale University Press.

Canale, M., and Swain, M. (1980). Theoretical bases of communicative approaches to second language teaching and testing. *Applied Linguistics 1,* (1): 1–47.

Chamot, A. U., and O'Malley, J. M. (1994). *The calla handbook: Implementing the cognitive academic language learning approach.* White Plains, NY: Addison Wesley.

Cummins, J. (2008). *ESL and second language learning web.* Retrieved January 2, 2008, from www.iteachilearn.com/cummins/.

Cummins, J. (2003). Challenging the construction of difference as deficit: Where are identity, intellect, imagination, and power in the new regime of truth? In P. Trifonas (Ed.), *Pedagogies of difference: Rethinking education for social change* (pp. 41–60). London: Routledge.

Cummins, J. (2000). *Language, power, and pedagogy: Bilingual children in the crossfire.* Clevedon, England: Multilingual Matters.

Cummins, J. (1981). *Bilingualism and minority language children.* Toronto: Ontario Institute for Studies in Education.

Cummins, J. (1979). Language functions and cognitive processing. In J. P. Das, J. Kirby, and R. F. Jarman (Eds.), *Simultaneous and successive processing* (pp. 175–185). New York: Academic Press.

Gee, J. P. (1996). *Social linguistics and literacies: Ideology in discourses* (2nd ed.). London: Taylor & Francis.

Kern, R. (2000). Notions of literacy. In R. Kern (Ed.), *Literacy and language teaching* (pp. 13–41). New York: Oxford University Press.

PACT. (2008). PACT consortium website. Retrieved January 6, 2009, from http://pacttpa .org.

Reading Institute for Academic Preparedness (RIAP). (2007). *RIAP orientation on academic language.* Retrieved December 10, 2007, from www.csun.edu/~rinstitute/Content/ instructional_materials/Orientation%202008.pdf.

Sato, M., and Curtis, M. (2005). *Making good choices: A support guide for the PACT teaching event.* Retrieved January 7, 2009, from http://www.srnleads.org/data/pdfs/pact.pdf.

Scarcella, R. C. (2003). *Accelerating academic English: A focus on the English learner.* Oakland: Regents of the University of California.

Stansbury, K. (2008). PACT 101: Deconstructing the teaching event. Presentation at PACT Consortium Conference, University of California at Santa Barbara, November 13.

Vygotsky, L. S. (1978). Interaction between learning and development. In M. Cole (Trans.), *Mind in society* (pp. 79–91). Cambridge, MA: Harvard University.

Vygotsky, L. S. (1962). *Thought and language.* Cambridge, MA: The MIT Press.

Wong Fillmore, L., and Snow, C. (2000). What teachers need to know about language. Washington, DC: ERIC Clearinghouse on Language and Linguistics. In the *Internet TESL Journal, 14.* Retrieved January 2, 2008, from http://iteslj.org.

Zwiers, J. (2008). *Building academic English: Essential practices for content classrooms.* San Francisco: Jossey-Bass.

CHAPTER 4

Scoring the Teaching Event

The PACT Teaching Event is scored by a 12-item rubric, known as a **scoring form,** which meets California Quality Standards of reliability and validity (Pecheone, 2008). Used by trained PACT scorers, the scoring form focuses on guiding questions and an analytic rubric to determine how well the candidate does in Planning, Instruction, Assessment, Reflection, and Academic Language in the Teaching Event.

Candidates must also supply a **Context** with Context Commentary on the demographics and needs of the specific target population of learners at the start of the Teaching Event. The Context Commentary, considered a foundational writing piece for the TE to come, is not scored but must be present. **Academic Language,** or the language demands of school, must be addressed in all tasks.

● The 12 Areas of the PACT Rubric

The 12 areas of the PACT rubric or scoring form appear within the five scored task areas of Planning, Instruction, Assessment, Reflection, and Academic Language of the Teaching Event, with guiding questions in each area. The Teacher Performance Expectations reflected in each task are listed in the rubric entries. Table 4.1 lists the 12 entries with their accompanying guiding questions. A list and discussion of the TPEs can be found in Chapter 1.

TABLE **4.1**

PACT Rubric Entries and Guiding Questions for Scoring the Teaching Event

Task	Area of Focus	Guiding Question
Planning	Establishing a Balanced Instructional Focus	*E1: How do the plans support student learning of strategies for understanding, interpreting, and responding to complex text? (TPEs 1, 4, 9)
	Making Content Accessible	E2: How do the plans make the curriculum accessible to the students in the class? (TPEs 1, 4, 5, 6, 7, 8, 9)
	Designing Assessments	E3: What opportunities do students have to demonstrate their understanding of the standards and learning objectives? (TPEs 1, 5, 11)
Instruction	Engaging Students in Learning	E4: How does the candidate actively engage students in their own understanding of how to understand, interpret, or respond to a complex text? (TPEs 1, 5, 11)
	Monitoring Student Learning During Instruction	E5: How does the candidate monitor student learning during instruction and respond to student questions, comments, and needs? (TPEs 2, 5)
Assessment	Analyzing Student Work During Instruction	E6: How does the candidate demonstrate an understanding of student performance with respect to standards/objectives? (TPEs 1, 3)
	Using Assessment to Inform Teaching	E7: How does the candidate use the analysis of student learning to propose next steps in instruction? (TPEs 3, 4)
	Using Feedback to Promote Student Learning	E8: What is the quality of feedback to students? (TPEs 3, 4)
Reflection	Monitoring Student Progress	E9: How does the candidate monitor student learning and make appropriate adjustments in instruction during the learning segment? (TPEs 2, 10, 12, 13)
	Reflecting on Learning	E10: How does the candidate use research, theory, and reflections on teaching and learning to guide practice? (TPEs 10, 11, 12, 13)
Academic Language	Understanding Language Demands	E11: How does the candidate describe the language demands of the learning tasks and assessments in relation to student language development? (TPEs 1, 4, 7, 8)
	Supporting Academic Language Development	E12: How do the candidate's planning, instruction, and assessment support academic language development? (TPEs 1, 4, 7, 8)

*E1 refers to English, scoring form item 1.
Source: http://pacttpa.org (PACT, 2008).

Using the Scoring Form in Multiple and Single Subjects

Teacher candidates are scored from Level 1 to Level 4, in each of the 12 areas of the scoring form. Generally speaking, Level 1 is low and not passing, and Level 4 is high and outstanding. According to PACT guidelines:

1. **Multiple-Subject candidates** must pass both the Teaching Event and all additional Multiple-Subject tasks.
2. Candidates pass the Teaching Event (in literacy or mathematics) if they pass all five rubric categories (Planning, Instruction, Assessment, Reflection, and Academic Language) AND have no more than two failing scores of "1" across tasks. To pass a category, candidates must have a majority (at least half) of passing scores within the category. In Planning, two out of three scores must be a "2" or higher; in Instruction, Assessment, Reflection, and Academic Language, one out of two scores must be a "2" or higher. Until piloting of the feedback rubric is completed, its score does not count toward passing.
3. Candidates pass the Teaching Event tasks in additional content areas (literacy/mathematics, history/social science, and science) if they have passing scores ("2" or higher) on more than half of the rubrics for the category corresponding to the task. The Planning category has three rubric scores, so this means that candidates can have at least two scores at "2" or higher. The Instruction and Assessment categories have two rubric scores, so both scores must be "2" or higher. (Until piloting of the feedback rubric is completed, its score does not count toward passing of the Assessment Task.) Programs choose the Teaching Event task to be completed in each content area (http://pacttpa.org [PACT, 2008]).

The Teaching Event Passing Standard for Single-Subject candidates states that **single-subject candidates** pass the Teaching Event "if they pass* all five rubric categories (Planning, Instruction, Assessment, Reflection, and Academic Language) AND have no more than two failing scores of "1" across tasks." (*Note: To pass a category, candidates must have a majority [at least half] of passing scores within the category. In Planning, two out of three scores must be a "2" or higher; in Instruction, Assessment, Reflection, and Academic Language, one out of two scores must be a "2" or higher. Until piloting of the feedback rubric is completed, its score does not count toward passing) (http://pacttpa.org [PACT, 2008]).

Remediation Opportunities for Candidates Who Do Not Pass PACT

PACT-aligned institutions have clear but varying procedures on how they address remediation—policies that must be approved in institutional plans submitted to CCTC. For example, Sacramento State's College of Education requires candidates to help develop a remediation plan and provides detailed procedures in its institution-specific PACT Handbook (2008) at http://edweb.csus.edu/pact/assets/pact_handbook.pdf.

The remediation process for single-subject candidates whose Teaching Events do not meet the passing standard is explained this way:

> If candidates fail the Teaching Event because they fail more than one task, OR have more than *3 "1"s across tasks, an entirely new Teaching Event must be re-taught and re-submitted. However, candidates who fail the Teaching Event because they failed only one task of the Teaching Event have the opportunity to resubmit specific individual tasks for a higher score. With the exception of the Reflection task, resubmitting a task involves more than simply re-writing/revising the commentary for an individual task. [*Note: For multiple subjects, no more than two "1s."] (www.pacttpa.org/ _files/Publications_and_Presentations/PACT_Technical_Report_March07 .pdf, p. 17)

The accompanying chart in Table 4.2 shows what tasks would need to be resubmitted for each task that is failed.

Appeals Procedure for Candidates Who Do Not Pass the Teaching Event

The PACT procedure for appeals is well-defined in its PACT Technical Report (2007, pp. 17–18) and includes information on time frames and rescoring:

1. Candidates who do not pass the Teaching Event and who choose not to remediate the score by resubmitting a task or an entire Teaching Event will have the right to appeal the failing score. . . . All Teaching Events not meeting the passing standard will have already been scored at least twice by trained scorers, and the evidence reviewed by the chief trainer . . . to ensure the reliability of scores. If the original double scores were con-

TABLE **4.2**

Resubmissions of Teaching Event Tasks

If the candidate fails this task . . .	Then these components must be resubmitted
Planning	Instructional context task; new series of lesson plans and instructional materials on a new topic; planning commentary
Instruction	Instructional context task; new video clips; new lesson plans for the lessons from which the video clips are drawn; instruction commentary
Assessment	Instructional context task; new student work samples; assessment commentary
Reflection	Revision of reflection commentary for previously taught Teaching Event; daily reflections cannot be revised
Academic Language	Instructional context task; new planning task + new instruction task

Source: http://www.pacttpa.org/_files/Publications_and_Presentations/PACT_Technical_Report_March07 .pdf [PACT Technical Report, 2007, p. 17]).

flicting, then the chief trainer will have independently scored the Teaching Event a third time to adjudicate the scores. If a candidate appeals the failing score, an investigation of the scorer training and scoring procedures at the local campus will be triggered.

2. If the investigation finds that the scorer training process at a local campus or scoring procedures were not in accordance with the scoring system as designed, the candidate then has the right to ask for a re-scoring of the Teaching Event by trained scorers external to the local program.

3. The re-scoring of the Teaching Event must occur within a month of the original appeal to allow the candidate time to re-submit a task or an entire Teaching Event should the re-scoring of the Teaching Event results in a failing score (www.pacttpa.org/_files/Publications_and_Presentations/ PACT_TechnicalReport_March07.pdf).

● **Training PACT Scorers**

The process of understanding, evaluating, and assessing teacher candidates with the PACT scoring form requires professional experience, training, expertise, and intensive training. In order to interpret and apply the 12 items and the 4 levels of the form, PACT scorers must participate in an intensive, typically 2-day training session at PACT-aligned institutions.

Scorers may be faculty, program coordinators, or university student teaching supervisors, but they are trained to score only in their subject area, such as music scorers for music, science scorers for science, and so forth. Scorers must also be *calibrated,* or aligned, with the scores of the official benchmark sample scores provided by the PACT consortium, before they can assess candidates' Teaching Events in their own teacher preparation programs. Once a year, scorers must also be recalibrated, to make sure their scores are still in line with state benchmark samples. Benchmark samples come from PACT-sponsored state scoring sessions, usually held twice a year and attended by participants from PACT-aligned institution teacher preparation programs.

Levels 1–4 on the PACT Teaching Event Scoring Form

Essentially, Level 1 is low and not passing, and Level 4 is high and outstanding, with 2 and above considered a passing score. On original National Assessment of Education Progress (NAEP) benchmark scores of 1–4 from the 1970s, scores 1 and 2 were considered not passing (below the line) and 3 and 4 were passing (above the line). After careful review and study, the PACT design team decided that some early adopter Teaching Events with scores of 2 contained passing and satisfactory elements. Thus, for the purposes of PACT scoring, *scores of 2 and above are in the passing range* (Stansbury, 2008).

The Guiding Questions on the PACT scoring forms are slightly different in each subject area and in multiple versus single subject for each of the 12 entries on the scoring form. The level descriptors for Levels 1–4 reflect the differences in guiding questions for each subject area. In its *Thinking Behind the Rubrics* document, PACT provides a detailed explanation of what each level means, including differences between adjacent levels (http://tracs.csun.edu/education/educ/pact/docs/THINKING_BEHIND_RUBRICS.doc) (CSUN, 2006).

The description of each level of the scoring form is not in the language of the rubric item itself and is not meant to be applied or even readily apparent to noneducators, nonspecialists, and those who have not been officially trained and calibrated as PACT scorers. In other words, nontrained individuals cannot and should not take the scoring form and attempt to apply its rubric item indicators without specialized PACT training.

The Big Ideas Behind the Rubrics

The big ideas behind each of the major scoring areas of Planning, Instruction, Assessment, Reflection, and Academic Language, and differences between levels can be found in Appendix A. These ideas assist scorers in understanding level indicators, as well as differentiating between and among the four scoring levels of 1–4 for each area.

Additional Information in the Scoring Form

The scoring form includes explanatory footnotes of some rubric items. Footnotes are provided to aid trained scorers, by providing additional definitions or examples that will assist them in evaluating the PACT Teaching Event. For example, in item E11 of the English language arts scoring form, footnotes add these other thoughts:

1. Text types can be oral (e.g., formal presentations, role play activities, arguments and counterarguments, partner or group discussions) and/or written (e.g., literary critiques, expository essays, narratives).
2. In addition to text types, examples might include understanding a teacher's oral presentation of information, responding to a question in class, listening to or reading directions, sharing information orally with a partner, or compiling information on a graphic organizer.
3. For example, common words that are new to English learners, synonyms used interchangeably, content terms with distinctive meanings from their everyday equivalents. (http://pacttpa.org [PACT, 2008])

Numerical Scores and Commentary in the Scoring Form

Scorers are required to give *numerical scores* and provide *textual evidence* through brief and specific comments, for the scores they give candidates in each of the 12 subcategories of the scoring form. An example of a Level 1 scorer comment in the planning area for English language arts might be, "Planned activities do not match stated standards/objectives, as a writing activity is planned for a geography map standard." An example of a Level 4 scorer comment in Academic Language for social studies might state, "Candidate identifies and explains features of the text types through a developmentally appropriate PowerPoint presentation and requires pupils to apply the featured text types to a writing activity on a current event."

Scorers are also encouraged to explain why a particular task is *not* a Level 1, 2, 3, or 4, using textual evidence from the candidate's Teaching Event to differentiate between scoring levels.

Examples of Candidates' Score Levels 1–4 from the Teaching Event

The four vignettes provided here from Teaching Events in **multiple-subject mathematics** demonstrate how candidates might answer a question on instruction and required video clips of teaching, with responses scored from Level 1 (low on scoring form) to Level 4 (high on scoring form). These examples are based on the prompt from Task 2, Instruction, on student engagement: "In the instruction seen in the clip(s), how did you further the students' knowledge and skills and engage them intellectually in understanding mathematical concepts and participating in mathematical discourse? Provide examples of both general strategies to address the needs of all of your students and strategies to address specific individual needs (TPEs 1, 2, 4, 5, 7, 11)."

1. *Candidate response at Level 1:*   In video clip 1, I gave the students a worksheet on going to the grocery store and estimating the total amount spent based on rounding product prices. One of the students asked me a question about rounding up, and the answer I gave seemed to confuse the class, so I need to prepare better next time for questions. In video clip 2, I wanted to ask the students in small groups more questions about why estimating is a good skill to have, but my cooperating teacher said my classroom management skills need more work and just to focus the discussions on the worksheet. Because groups spent too much time socializing, they didn't finish the assignment.

2. *Candidate response at Level 2:*   During the class discussion in video clip 1, I used a "trip to the grocery store" worksheet on estimating the total bill by rounding the cost of products. On my desk, I had examples of products students might buy at the store, such as shampoo, a candy bar, and a power drink, and I asked students first to guess how much they cost. Certain students wanted to answer all the questions, so I need to find ways to engage all the students, not just a few, in the whole-group discussion. In video clip 2, I structured the activities, so students moved from independent tasks to cooperative learning, working in assigned teams of four to complete the grocery store worksheet. Each student had a role and was held accountable for individual learning, but some groups were off-task and needed refocusing. Also, students asked for clearer directions on how to complete their individual assignments within the group structure.

3. *Candidate response at Level 3:* In both video clips, I used open-ended questions and extended wait time, so that anyone (not just the student with the right answer) could reflect on and respond to the questions raised by the "trip to the grocery store" estimation worksheet. I brought in current examples of estimation from magazine and newspaper ads and asked students to provide their own examples. In discussing the worksheet and ad examples, I used specific feedback and built on other students' responses, such as, "Isabel makes a good point about rounding being a good skill for everyday shopping and going to restaurants. Can anyone else suggest another situation in which estimation and rounding might be helpful?" When students answered questions in the whole-group discussion, I asked them to tell how (give evidence of how) they arrived at their responses. I structured the cooperative learning task with assigned roles and questions for all team members that required each person to submit responses for certain sections of the worksheet at the end of the activity.

4. *Candidate response at Level 4:* In both video clips, I sought to maximize student engagement and discussion, so I could monitor how much students were learning, and whether they could explain their thinking. In video clip 1, I used PowerPoint with colorful graphics I had found on estimation/rounding at the grocery store. I had students first guess the price of a pictured product then estimate its cost by rounding. To elicit student thinking, I placed a "thinking break" (open-ended question) on every few slides for thought and discussion, such as "How can estimation/rounding help you in everyday life?" or "Have you ever seen a friend or family member use estimation?" I required all students to write a brief answer to each question and submit their answers at the end of the PowerPoint presentation. I also used similar, open-ended questions in a whole-group discussion. This strategy helped focus student thinking and helped me monitor their understanding of the estimation and rounding concepts. During the cooperative learning activity in video clip 2, I built on student input to guide improvement; to assist learners in breaking down the worksheet questions into manageable parts; and to assign all group members a role and task (for individual accountability for the worksheet) to be submitted at the end of the group work. Each cooperative team also had to generate at least one question of its own on estimation and rounding, to be shared with the rest of the class. I used the research of Johnson and Johnson (1984, 2000) and Kagan (1968, 2008) to inform my monitoring of student learning by using the major, recommended steps of cooperative learning activities. Students responded positively to both the whole-group thinking questions and the cooperative learning assignment.

Brief Analysis of Vignettes

The Level 1 candidate response in the vignettes shows that students are following instructions and completing the activity, but unclear directions limit student opportunities for understanding. The candidate at Level 1 fails to structure the cooperative learning task effectively and may only be interacting with a few students. Student confusion about the activity and lack of focus in the learning environment interfere with student learning.

The Level 2 candidate provides students with strategies relative to the content and attempts to engage students in the learning task. Some groups were off-task and needed refocusing on the assignment.

At Level 3, the candidate structures the strategies to engage students intellectually in the learning task and integrates some attention to individual learner needs. The candidate builds on student responses but does not identify strategies as intentional and needs to build a rationale for them.

The Level 4 candidate explicitly identifies strategies for intellectual engagement, clearly recognizable in the video clips. The candidate informs the range of instructional choices with research from intellectual experts and demonstrates an understanding of why selected strategies work with students.

In these examples of responses to the PACT Teaching Event Task 2, Instruction, candidates are scored on the quality and depth of thought and analysis, rather than the length of their response. Candidates with longer responses, however, tend to include more facts, details, and examples to support their ideas. Appendix A addresses the big ideas behind the rubric in greater detail.

The Role of Bias in Scoring the Teaching Event

Certainly any task taken on by human scorers will retain a residue of their individual biases, preferences, likes, and dislikes. PACT scorers are especially and specifically trained to be aware of biases in reading the Teaching Event and watching the video clips. For example, professional dress is encouraged for teacher candidates, but scorers cannot downgrade a student teacher who is dressed in jeans or who has bright purple hair.

Scoring keeps coming back to the rubric (i.e., anything outside the parameters of the scoring form should not be considered or evaluated). Some scorers are sticklers for grammar and mechanics, and although intelligible writing is important, the Teaching Event artifacts and video clips are scored strictly according to the descriptors of the scoring form.

In the training of scorers, **biases** are described in this way:

1. We all have biases, as we are influenced by our preferences and experiences.
2. Some biases, based on research, theoretical perspective, or instructional experiences, are simply an outgrowth of our professional knowledge.
3. Educators have preferences about the kind of teaching they like and the contexts with which they are familiar.
4. Scorers' biases may be triggered by the quality of writing, technical quality of materials submitted, quality of instructional materials submitted, candidates not following directions or missing items, and liking or not liking the particular grade level or assignment.
5. The same situation in a single Teaching Event may trigger different kinds of bias in different scorers. (http://pacttpa.org [PACT, 2008])

Further cautions about bias, both about candidates and scorers, include reminders that:

1. Some candidates are better writers than others, but great writing does not necessarily mean great teaching (and the inverse is true).
2. Scorers should not be distracted by the technical features of the Teaching Event, such as the audio or video quality of the video clips.
3. Candidates who use commercially prepared instructional materials, rather than authentic materials, may receive unfair credit for their professional products.
4. Inferences about a candidate's undescribed intentions not documented by the artifacts and video clips are unwarranted and should not be considered in scoring.

5. Candidates may fail to take into account the pupils' prior achievement and language proficiency, making it appear the pupils learned content easily or had undue challenges.
6. Candidates may not teach the same way scorers would under the same circumstances.
7. Candidates may shine in one area and be somewhat lackluster in another, putting scorers on an evaluative emotional rollercoaster.
8. One scorer may interpret the rubrics strictly, while another gives the candidate some latitude in the task area. (http://pacttpa.org [PACT, 2008])

Acquiring the PACT Teaching Event Scoring Forms

PACT scoring forms are currently password-protected on the PACT consortium website, http://pacttpa.org. You may contact the consortium about obtaining materials or receive them as a qualified candidate in a PACT-aligned teacher preparation program.

Research Basis for the PACT Scoring Form

Interrater reliability, content validity, concurrent validity, decision consistency, and a bias and fairness review as applied to the PACT teaching event are all discussed in the Introduction. The Introduction chapter also discusses the latest research on teacher performance assessment, including the findings that support the PACT scoring form.

● Summary

The beauty of the PACT Teaching Event rubric is that each candidate is assessed by trained scorers, on preestablished criteria deeply rooted in the best research available on teacher performance assessment. Using a scoring form that focuses on guiding questions and an analytic rubric, scorers evaluate candidates in 12 subcategories of 5 tasks: Planning, Instruction, Assessment, Reflection, and Academic Language.

Scorers receive in-depth training to assess the Teaching Event, with special attention given to providing textual evidence, called *comments,* for the numerical scores they give, and for the reasons a score achieves one level but not another. Taken together, the scores and comments on the 12 subcategories of the 5 major tasks of the Teaching Event provide a reliable and detailed analysis of a candidate's ability in delivering the unified learning segment and acumen in fulfilling the specified requirements.

Candidates submitting the PACT Teaching Event are evaluated both on their successful completion of tasks and depth of response to tasks, with connections made between and among tasks. Artifacts, commentaries, and video clips provide a well-rounded view of the teaching candidate in the areas identified by education experts as essential to quality teaching performance.

References

California State University Northridge (CSUN). (2006). *Thinking behind rubrics.* Retrieved November 29, 2007, from http://tracs.csun.edu/education/educ/pact/docs/THINKING_BEHIND_RUBRICS.doc, 2006.

PACT. (2008). *PACT consortium website.* Retrieved January 6, 2009, from http://pacttpa.org.

PACT Handbook. (2008). Sacramento State College of Education. Retrieved May 7, 2009, from http://edweb.csus.edu/pact/assets/pact_handbook.pdf.

PACT Technical Report. (2007). *Technical report of the performance assessment for California teachers (PACT): Summary of validity and reliability studies for the 2003–04 pilot year.* Retrieved February 24, 2009, from www.pacttpa.org/_files/Publications_and_Presentations/PACT_Technical_Report_March07.pdf, pp. 17–18.

Pecheone, R. (2008). *The thinking behind PACT: Performance assessment for California teachers.* Retrieved January 6, 2008, from http://pacttpa.org/_files/Publications_and_Presentations/PACT.ppt.

Stansbury, K. (2008). PACT 101: Deconstructing the teaching event. Presentation at PACT Consortium Conference, University of California at Santa Barbara, November 13.

CHAPTER 5

Next Steps for PACT

What does the Teaching Event tell PACT-aligned institutions about their candidates' teaching performance? Aligned with the California Teaching Performance Expectations, state standards, and curricular frameworks, the PACT Teaching Event shows that candidates can "demonstrate their readiness for a full-time teaching assignment" (Stansbury, 2006, p. 1). The PACT Teaching Event is seen as a robust, viable instrument for research on teaching performance and teaching practice data, especially in regard to *preparing preservice candidates to be high-quality teachers.*

For well over a decade, researchers at Stanford University and other institutions have advocated standards-based teacher assessment linked to school reform as a system for building the capacity of teachers. Their research strongly indicates that linking teaching standards with student standards helps focus and coordinate state reforms to address knowledge, skills, and abilities needed by teachers to enhance student learning (Pecheone & Stansbury, 1996). This perspective has gained momentum over time and ultimately resulted in the development of the PACT Teaching Event.

The PACT Teaching Event requires candidates to provide *documented evidence of their teaching and student learning,* including lesson plans, student work samples, teacher feedback, videotapes of teaching, and structured reflection and commentaries on the decisions they make regarding teaching practices. PACT researchers and participating institutions are using that evidence to inform discussions in several areas. Discussions about modifications of course content, structures, and roles, including structural changes in teacher education programs, occur as a result of the implementation and scoring of the PACT Teaching Event. Changes are not made for the sake of change within credentialing programs but are designed to build the best teacher preparation programs possible, based on the most reliable performance assessment available (Pecheone & Chung, 2006).

Research suggests that "the PACT performance assessment can be used in teacher education as a valid measure of individual teacher competence for the purpose of teacher licensure and as a powerful tool for teacher learning and program improvement" (Pecheone & Chung, 2006). Portfolio assessments are extending the culture of evidence in teacher licensing to identify effective teachers through more valid means and to bring about higher quality induction and professional development experiences, especially for beginning teachers (Pecheone & Chung, 2006).

Ongoing and longitudinal research is recommended by educational experts in these areas of teacher performance assessment, including the PACT Teaching Event:

1. Portfolio assessments as evidence
2. Beginning teacher effectiveness
3. Examination of correlates of PACT Teaching Event scores
4. Other tests, grades, supervisory scores for individual candidates
5. Program features related to performance in different areas
6. Following candidates into first year of teaching
7. Teaching practices
8. Student learning outcomes
9. Contributions of PACT Embedded Signature Assignments (ESAs) specific to individual teacher program preparation programs—such as community studies, child case studies, and analyses of student learning—to judgments about teacher competence
10. PACT as a valid, reliable, unbiased, and fair teacher performance assessment (Pecheone & Chung, 2006)

Next steps in the implementation of the PACT TE must continue to provide participating campuses with the opportunity to examine program differences in candidate performance within and across credential programs. Member institutions also have an opportunity to collaborate, in order to address areas of candidate weaknesses and ways to improve those areas, including best practices and the research that underlies instructional decisions. Dialogue on the design, scoring, and implementation processes of the assessment must continue within and across programs about what constitutes effective teaching at the preservice level (Pecheone & Chung, 2006).

Faculty and student teaching supervisors need to persist in meaningful discussions about what candidates should know and be able to do, both in the PACT Teaching Event and in their credential program. Teacher preparation programs must persevere in examining the kinds of support and preparation they provide to candidates. The PACT TE should be viewed as an instrument of accountability and as "a well-designed performance assessment system [with] the potential to be a powerful tool in providing meaningful feedback to individual candidates and to evaluate the impact of teacher education programs" (Pecheone & Chung, 2006, p. 33).

Next steps also include studying effects of the recent convergence of three key factors: the development of the PACT Teaching Event as a performance assessment, electronic portfolio systems, and new scoring software. The effects of electronic portfolio systems and scoring software on scorer training and portfolio evaluation must be examined in terms of their costs, validity, and reliability (Melnick & Pullin, 2000; Moss, 1998; Youngs, Odden, & Porter, 2003; all in Pecheone, 2005, p. 171).

Do educators have conclusive evidence that teachers actually improve their practices as a result of participating in the PACT Teaching Event? Do education researchers understand all the critical aspects of teacher assessment that influence teacher learning, including contexts, support, pupil learning outcomes, and standards-based teaching practices? How do constraints on teaching practices, such as scripted programs and other district or state curricular decisions, affect both practice and assessment? What can education experts learn about preservice teaching practice, after decades of focus on teachers already on the job? Next steps for study of teacher performance assessments must consider all these issues and any others that emerge to inform the discussion.

● Additional Issues for Further Study

Other PACT-related issues indicate a need for longitudinal studies to address these questions:

1. Is PACT a valid and reliable predictor of teaching success?
2. What is the cost factor, the monetary implications of campuses implementing PACT?
3. Are "poor" teachers being weeded out by the assessment?
4. How is PACT being received by the California Commission on Teacher Credentialing (CCTC)?
5. Have any institutions dropped out of the PACT consortium, and if so, why?
6. How do PACT-assessed teachers compare with CalTPA teachers?
7. How can preservice teachers assessed by PACT continue its kind of implementation and reflection features as beginning teachers?
8. Could the results of PACT be used as an action research project for beginning teachers, not just as an assessment of preservice teachers?
9. Could PACT become a nationally available model of teacher performance assessment?

Summary

While California's rich history of educational reform is still being written, PACT may be seen one day as a watershed event in teacher performance assessment for preservice teachers. Unlike other education movements in the state, it has provided both a catalyst for change and a lightning rod for reform. The PACT Teaching Event's focus on a deep, structured analysis of the pillars of teaching—Planning, Instruction, Assessment, and Reflection, with attention to Context and Academic Language—captures all the key pieces of research available on teacher quality, best practices, and performance assessment.

In the Teaching Event, beginning teachers must provide documented evidence through artifacts, commentaries, and videotaped teaching that demonstrates knowledge of and skills in standards-based, developmentally appropriate teaching practices and learning outcomes. The resulting portfolio assessment of written work and teacher videos offers rich opportunities to education experts for systematic research on both the assessment and its effects on candidates and teacher preparation programs.

It is not enough to talk about or demand teacher quality. Teacher quality must be defined and assessed through instruments such as the PACT

Teaching Event, so that preservice candidates—and the teacher programs that prepare them—can understand what subject-specific and pedagogical knowledge, skills, and dispositions effective teachers need to acquire, develop, and apply to successful classroom practice. PACT implementers hope to create the best teacher performance assessment—for the best teachers—ever developed.

References

Pecheone, R. (2005). *Overview of elementary literacy teaching event.* Retrieved May 11, 2007, from http://www.pacttpa.org/_files/Publications_and_Presentations/Appendixes_A-D.pdf, p. 171.

Pecheone, R., and Chung, R. (2006). Evidence in teacher education: The performance Assessment for California Teachers (PACT). *Journal of Teacher Education 57,* 22–36. Retrieved June 11, 2007, from http://pacttpa.org/_files/Publications_and_Presentations/PACT_Evidence_Teacher_Ed_JTE.pdf.

Pecheone, R., and Stansbury, K. (1996). Connecting teacher assessment and school reform. *Elementary School Journal* 97, (2): 163–177.

Stansbury, K. (2006). English language arts teaching event candidate handbook 2008–09. Paper presented at PACT Consortium Conference, University of California at Santa Barbara, November 13.

The Big Ideas
Behind the Rubrics

Task	Focus Area	Big Ideas	Differences among Levels
Planning	Establishing a balanced instructional focus	1. One vs. multi-dimensional central focus 2. Connections between different types of knowledge in the content areas 3. Progression of learning tasks 4. Deep understandings of the central focus	**At Level 1,** the standards/objectives, learning tasks, and assessments focus exclusively on one type of knowledge to the exclusion of any others. **At Level 2,** one type of knowledge is very dominant, with only superficial, fleeting, or inconsistent attention given to other types of knowledge. **At Level 3,** there are clear connections between the various types of knowledge. "Clear" means that the connections go beyond the superficial. The daily set of standards/objectives, learning tasks, and assessments work together to build a progressive understanding of the content. **At Level 4,** the connections happen for both the learning tasks *and* the assessment tasks. In addition, the progression provides students opportunities to deepen their understanding of the central focus of the learning segment. **Special Note for Elementary Literacy only:** In Elementary Literacy, a lack of focus can be achieved through a learning segment which is centered on integrated instruction, but that does not focus on *literacy* learning.

(continues)

Task	Focus Area	Big Ideas	Differences among Levels
Planning	Making content accessible	1. Significant content inaccuracies 2. Relationship of students' experiential backgrounds, interests, or prior learning to the standards/objectives 3. Forms of student support 4. Access to grade-level literacy standards and objectives	**At Level 1,** there are significant errors in the content being taught. Aspects of the students' experiential backgrounds, interests, or prior learning are reflected in the plans and have a superficial relationship with the standards/objectives, so the connections aren't very useful in helping students learn the content. **At Level 2,** this relationship is used in the plan to help move students toward meeting the learning objectives. Any errors present do not significantly disadvantage students in future learning. In addition, there is at least one general strategy for addressing the needs of students who often have difficulty, e.g., the candidate plans to circulate while students are working and help those who are struggling. **At Level 3,** the plans not only draw on students' prior learning, but they also draw on students' experiences or interests to help them meet standards and reach the learning objectives appropriate for their grade level. These candidates *structure* support strategies to help students gain access to the grade-level curriculum. For example, if heterogeneous grouping is planned, there is a process to ensure that students do not just copy the work of others but actively engage in developing their own understanding.

Task	Focus Area	Big Ideas	Differences among Levels
Planning (cont.)			**At Level 4,** the candidates' plans and commentary suggest an understanding of how to meet varied student needs in a classroom. This is not limited to English learners or special needs students, although these students have specific needs that often require differentiation or strategic teaching decisions. The candidates may identify other types of student needs that are being considered during planning, e.g., students who are reluctant to participate in discussions, students who already know the content or who learn it more quickly than other students. There are two approaches to accommodating particular student needs: (1) differentiating instruction, where different instruction is planned to address the needs; and (2) strategic teaching decisions, where instruction is planned that simultaneously addresses multiple needs, perhaps with scaffolding or additional support for students who need it. (*Note:* The candidates need not be meeting *every* student's learning needs, but there should be evidence that there are reasonable strategies for meeting both the needs of students as a class and a variety of distinct needs of individuals or subgroups.)

(continues)

Task	Focus Area	Big Ideas	Differences among Levels
Planning	Designing assessments	1. Match standards/ objectives and assessments 2. Type of student understandings measured by assessments 3. Productive/ receptive modalities 4. Accommodation of special student needs	**At Level 1:** A significant mismatch exists between one or more assessments and the content and skills inherent in the learning tasks described in the plans. At least one assessment requires knowledge and skills that go *far* beyond those described in the context commentary or taught during the learning segment. The mismatch should be major, and at least one of the assessments does not match the learning objectives identified as being assessed. **At Level 2,** the standards and objectives, instruction, and assessments match. However, this match is clear only at a surface-level of understanding. **At Level 3,** the assessments clearly allow students to display their understanding or skill in some depth relative to the students' developmental level, the short length of the learning segment, and the amount of time students have been working on the particular concept, skill, or understanding as described in the standards/objectives. In addition, both students' ability to communicate their own understandings and skills (productive modalities, e.g., writing, speaking, drawing/graphing) and their understanding of content communicated by others (receptive modalities, e.g., reading, listening, viewing) are assessed. **At Level 4,** assessments reflect a deliberate design, changes in the assessment instrument or method of administration, or options offered to address the special needs of one or more students who otherwise would be limited in the ability to demonstrate the expected understandings and skills.

Task	Focus Area	Big Ideas	Differences among Levels
Instruction	Engaging students in learning	1. Student opportunities to engage in developing their own understandings 2. Focus of clip(s) 3. Problematic classroom management that interferes with learning	**At Level 1,** the students are following instructions and completing the activity, but there is something that limits students' opportunities to develop their own understanding of the required focus of the video clip. This may be due to the content of the questions asked by the teacher or the nature of the activity that the students are asked to do. The teacher may only be interacting with a few of the students without attempting to engage the others. Level 1 also includes candidates whose classrooms are so disruptive or disrespectful of students and their ideas that the environment consistently interferes with student learning, as well as candidates whose video clip(s) do not reflect the required focus. **At Level 2,** the strategies offer students opportunities to *engage* with the content relative to the required focus of the clip(s). Not all students may be actually doing so, but the teacher attempts to engage students in the learning task (not just participate) that can be identified within the clip(s). **At Level 3,** the strategies are structured to engage students intellectually in the learning task(s) and incorporate some attention to students as individuals, i.e., who the students are, their language needs, or other specific learning needs. These strategies may be weakly implemented and/or not explicitly identified by the candidate as intentional. **At Level 4,** candidates need to explicitly identify strategies for intellectual engagement, either in the Instruction commentary or earlier in the Planning Task. The strategies should be clearly recognizable in the video clip(s).

(continues)

Task	Focus Area	Big Ideas	Differences among Levels
Instruction	Monitoring student learning during instruction	1. Strategies for monitoring student understanding 2. Candidate responses 3. Significant content inaccuracies	**At Level 1,** candidates display one or more inaccuracies that negatively impact student learning and scores. Alternatively, candidates who primarily monitor student learning by asking yes/no or other types of simple questions (either orally or through written materials) don't require much thinking on the part of students (i.e., surface-level questions). **At Level 2,** candidates are requiring students to think to respond during the activities shown in the video clip(s). This student thinking is grounded in knowledge of facts, skills, conventions, etc., and is not just providing unsupported opinions. Candidates respond to students in ways that are "reasonable" attempts to improve student understanding. *Reasonable* means that candidates are attempting to apply instructional strategies and are making an effort to direct students to some content understanding that requires thinking, not just responding with prior knowledge or just parroting back what has been said previously. The strategies that candidates are using may or may not be working, but their purpose is clearly to get students to think more deeply. These candidates have more to learn about using strategies effectively, but they are making a reasonable effort to get students to think. **At Level 3,** candidates are using the responses to guide what they do next, in such a way that they are building student understanding. It is evident from candidates' responses that they

Task	Focus Area	Big Ideas	Differences among Levels
Instruction (cont.)			are evaluating the students' responses and making decisions accordingly to support students in developing the desired understanding or skills. **At Level 4,** candidates are making thinking visible so that students understand the reasoning behind at least some responses, modeling thinking processes or helping students understand what is important to notice and talk about in the content area.
Assessment	Analyzing student work from an assessment	1. Student errors, skills, and understanding 2. Patterns in student performance	**At Level 1,** either the assessment criteria and/or analysis are not aligned with the standards/objectives identified as being assessed or evidence in the student work samples is not consistent with the conclusions drawn. This may be due to either flaws in the assessment instrument chosen or to flaws in the analysis. An "analysis" that does not address student performance, e.g., a description of instruction leading to the assessment, though not referenced in the rubric, also merits a Level 1 rating. **At Level 2,** the candidates' analyses are a listing of students' successes and errors or misunderstandings which are related to the relevant standards/objectives. However, the candidates make few attempts to use these to understand what the student might have been thinking or doing as they produced their responses. A Level 2 analysis also identifies a few general characteristics of student learning or performances that constitute differing degrees of attainment of the learning objectives.

(continues)

Task	Focus Area	Big Ideas	Differences among Levels
Assessment (cont.)			**At Level 3,** the analysis uses student errors as an indicator of student understanding. It goes beyond cataloguing successes and errors/misunderstandings on the assessment instrument to describe patterns, either for individuals or for subgroups of students, that shed light on the extent of student understanding or skill. In the case of errors or misunderstandings, the candidates use patterns to probe for specific sources of misunderstandings, e.g., lack of understanding of a particular concept or procedure, inattention to detail. The pattern for individuals may be within the work sample or over time, using other sources of evidence and connecting them to the performance in the work sample provided. These patterns are strategically chosen to gain insight into possible intervention points to address student errors or misunderstandings in order for them to make progress relative to the standards/objectives.
			At Level 4, the candidates add partial understandings. The candidates are able to recognize incomplete progress toward the standards/objectives and identify parts that the student has mastered as well as additional parts that the student(s) need to work on. The detail and clarity of the analysis indicates a depth of understanding of student performance and more comprehensive consideration of various dimensions of student performance than analyses scored at Level 3.

Task	Focus Area	Big Ideas	Differences among Levels
Assessment	Using assessment to Inform teaching	1. Focusing for next steps 2. Basis for next steps	**At Level 1,** (a) the next steps are either vaguely described, e.g., "more support" with no details as to the focus of support or how it would be offered; (b) the next steps are not very closely related to any of the conclusions drawn in the analysis; or (c) the analysis was so flawed that the next steps are not suitable to meet student needs indicated by the student work samples. **At Level 2,** the next steps are based on broadly defined patterns of performance, and are focused on student misunderstandings, errors, or a need for greater challenge. **At Level 3,** the next steps are more targeted to individuals or groups and the needs addressed are more specifically defined. The next steps are based on a deeper level of analysis that distinguishes needs of individuals or subgroups. **At Level 4,** the next steps are very targeted, in such a way as to indicate a clear understanding of the key features of content and/or language standards/objectives as well as how to use knowledge about students to help them learn.

(continues)

Task	Focus Area	Big Ideas	Differences among Levels
Assessment	Using feed-back to promote student learning	1. Feedback to students 2. Strong under-standing of stu-dents, content, and language goals	**At Level 1,** feedback is general and provides little guidance for improve-ment related to learning objectives, or the feedback contains significant inaccuracies. **At Level 2,** the feedback identifies what was done well and areas for improvement related to specific learn-ing objectives. **At Level 3,** specific feedback helps the student understand what s/he has done well, and gives suggestions to guide improvement. **At Level 4,** specific comments are supportive and prompt analysis by the student of his/her own performance. The feedback shows strong under-standing of students as individuals in reference to the content and language objectives they are trying to meet.
Reflection	Monitoring student progress	1. Monitoring student learning 2. Adjustments in instruction	**At Level 1,** student learning is not con-sistently monitored. These reflections often make global assertions like "Went well today" without considering if this was true for all students or offer-ing an observation of student perform-ance that suggests what led to that conclusion. Alternatively, candidates may indicate that some students are having difficulty or, conversely, that students are easily learning the mate-rial, without considering any implica-tions for the future lessons planned. **At Level 2,** the reflections on student learning resemble a list of what stu-dents could or could not successfully do during each lesson. The reflections may also include considerations of

Task	Focus Area	Big Ideas	Differences among Levels
Reflection (cont.)			time management or problematic student behavior that are independent of the consequences for student learning. However, the modifications of plans is limited either to procedures for implementing activities (e.g., better estimating what can be done during the time period or being more clear about what is needed to complete a learning task) or to going over the same materials in the same way for students who did not understand.
			At Level 3, there may also be consideration of the use of instructional time to complete learning tasks, improving directions, or other classroom management issues, but a focus on student progress is also evident. Candidates' reflections are connected across lessons or associated with specific standards/objectives to give a notion of the degree of progress toward meeting the standards/objectives. At least some adjustments to instruction focus on specific learning needs, both for individuals and one or more groups of students (which may include the whole class).
			At Level 4, the adjustments are well targeted at features of student learning for the learning segment that are most central in helping students meet the standards/objectives. These features differ among content areas, but are described in general terms in the rubric.

(continues)

Task	Focus Area	Big Ideas	Differences among Levels
Reflection	Reflecting on learning	1. Grounding of reflections in research and theory 2. Basis for changes in teaching practice	**At Level 1,** candidates cite a theory or research finding that has nothing to do with the strategy, event, or student performance the candidates are reflecting on (e.g., using Piaget's stage theory as a rationale for group work) or to offer an erroneous interpretation or explanation of a research finding or theory (e.g., an assertion that Bloom's taxonomy suggests that students cannot analyze or evaluate ideas unless they have mastered basic skills in the content area). These errors should be egregious and not subtle. Alternatively, there is little or no evidence that candidates can make appropriate connections between their teaching practice and student learning. **At Level 2,** the reflections are consistent with theory and research, at a general level, but they are not closely connected. The candidates do not seem to be using research and theory to make sense of experience, but more searching for a way to apply familiar research and theory in some fashion. Candidates also identify changes in their teaching practice to solve some problem that they identified. These changes reflect an assumption about how their teaching affected student learning. You may know, based on experience, that either this assumption is not the most likely or the change that they suggest is not likely to work. However, the key idea is that the assumption or the change would seem reasonable to candidates, given their limited experience at this stage of their teaching careers in applying what they have learned.

Task	Focus Area	Big Ideas	Differences among Levels
Reflection (cont.)			**At Level 3,** candidates use principles of theory and research to make sense of what they observed about their students and their learning. This should be explicit (thought not necessarily detailed) in the reflections.
			At Level 4, there is a closer connection between the research/theory cited, knowledge of students, and knowledge of content. The changes proposed address the learning of both individuals and groups of students and are tied to the standards/objectives for the learning segment.
Academic Language	Understanding language demands	1. Language demands of learning and assessment tasks 2. Students' language strengths and needs	**At Level 1,** description reflects a superficial understanding of language development and language demands. The description of language demands of tasks is shallow. The discussion of student language development focuses on errors easily recognizable to non-educators, such as spelling and grammar, but not patterns of spelling and grammatical structures related to the texts used in the learning segment. Another way to achieve a Level 1 score is to provide a list of new vocabulary without any explanation of why these words might be challenging for students.
			At Level 2, virtually the only language demand that candidates describe that goes beyond grammar and spelling is related to vocabulary, and the candidates briefly indicate why these might be challenging for students, e.g., different meanings of familiar words.
			At Level 3, candidates go beyond identifying vocabulary as the sole

(continues)

Task	Focus Area	Big Ideas	Differences among Levels
Academic Language (cont.)			language demand to include challenging features of subject-specific text types or more general language demands related to routine tasks in the classroom. The discussion of students' language development relative to these demands includes student strengths as well as developmental needs.
			At Level 4, candidates also identify and explain features of the text types or other demands that make them challenging for a student or a group.
Academic Language	Supporting academic language development	Scaffolding or support for academic language	**At Level 1,** either little language support is provided to address student needs in relationship to the language demands of tasks or the content and/or language is so oversimplified so that little development in either content or language takes place.
			At Level 2, candidates identify specific strategies for closing identified language gaps between student levels of development and the demands of learning tasks and assessments. However, while these strategies allow access to content, there is an *absence* of strategies that are specifically targeted at developing language proficiency. Examples of such strategies that provide access to content without developing specific academic language include using pictures in the absence of accompanying language or pairing English learners with a more fluent English speaker who shares the primary language with no provision for the more fluent student doing

Task	Focus Area	Big Ideas	Differences among Levels
Academic Language (cont.)			more than serving as a translator to help the less fluent student through the learning task.
			At Level 3, the scaffolds and supports offered to bridge gaps in needs relative to demands not only provide access to content understanding but also target language development. Strategies to help give students understand curriculum content that does not build English proficiency may be present as well to build content understandings. However, at Level 3 explicit strategies to develop academic language must be present.
			At Level 4, there is also an explanation of the instructional strategies and how they address the language gap between what the students can currently do and what the learning task requires them to do.

Note: The academic language rubrics differ from the previous rubrics in that they are designed to draw from evidence across all tasks.

Source: http://tracs.csun.edu/education/educ/pact/docs/THINKING_BEHIND_RUBRICS.doc (CSUN, 2006, p. 6); http://pacttpa.org (PACT, 2008).

Index